R. Martin lith. 26 Long Acre.

VIEW FROM THE INTERIOR OF SOCOTRA.

Published by Henry Colburn, Great Marlborough St. 1840.

# TRAVELS

TO THE

# CITY OF THE CALIPHS,

ALONG THE SHORES

OF THE

# PERSIAN GULF

AND

# THE MEDITERRANEAN.

INCLUDING A

VOYAGE TO THE COAST OF ARABIA,

AND A

TOUR ON THE ISLAND OF SOCOTRA.

By J. R. WELLSTED, Esq., F.R.S., F.R.A.S., &c. &c.

AUTHOR OF "TRAVELS IN ARABIA."

IN TWO VOLUMES.

VOL. II.



LONDON:
HENRY COLBURN, PUBLISHER,
GREAT MARLBOROUGH STREET.

1840.

Printed by J. L. Cox and Sons, 75, Great Queen Street,
Lincoln's-Inn Fields.

# CONTENTS

OF

# THE SECOND VOLUME.

---

## MESOPOTAMIA, AND THE SHORES OF THE MEDITERRANEAN.

---

### CHAPTER I.

Page

Arrive at Tripoli—Author falls in love—Customs of various Countries—Quit Tripoli—Reflections ... 1

### CHAPTER II.

Engage a Servant—Sail for Cyprus—Tyre—Cushites—Himyaritic Writing identical with the Language of Job—Still a spoken Language—Queen Sheba—Concluding Remarks ... ... ... ... .. 17

### CHAPTER III.

Servant's History—Early Miseries—Falls in love—Visit of his Master—Evasion ... ... ... 42

## CHAPTER IV.

Page

Enter the Orontes—proceed to Antioch—quit the River—Storm in the Gulf of Scanderoon—Phosphorescent appearance of Sea—Boat capsized—Author's perilous situation—arrive at Scanderoon—its pestilential Climate—Incident—again visit Antioch—Description of that City—rejoin Jim—monstrous Fish—open a Shop, and retail Shoes and Sandals—hasty Departure—Land Travelling ... ... ... ... 59

## CHAPTER V.

Proceed to Khalat el Hassan—Reflections—Imprisonment for Debt unknown in the East—Taken as a Spy—Sentenced to Death—Pardoned, and quit the Town—Return to Aleppo—Valley of the Orontes—Theological Discussion—Enter Aleppo—Frequency of Earthquakes—Character of Inhabitants—Education—Propriety of Demeanour—their Children ... 76

## CHAPTER VI.

Effects of Earthquakes—Dread entertained by the Inhabitants—Greek Lady—her Daughters—Author joins their circle—fearful Convulsion—Apathy of the Moollahs—a Prediction—People return to the City—Visitation of a second Shock—Escape to a Cypress Tree—quit the Tree, and seek the Females—meet them in the Gardens—quit for Damascus—Colonel Chesney, and Steam Navigation *viâ* Euphrates—arrive at Bagdad, and quit for India ... ... ... 93

# A VOYAGE TO THE COAST OF ARABIA,

AND

# TOUR ON THE ISLAND OF SOCOTRA.

## CHAPTER I.

Page

Maritime Geography—Captain Owen—Sir Charles Malcolm—his Encouragement of Geographical Pursuits—East-India Company—Discovery of Ancient Inscriptions—Author arrives at Cape Isolette—Effects of Terrestrial Refraction—Phosphorescent Appearance of the Sea—Fluctuation in the Temperature—Currents within the Gulf of Aden—Arrival at Morebat—its Prosperity—Seid Mahomet Akyl—Ferocity of Bedowins—Arrival at Kisseen—Visit to its Chief ... ... ... ... ... ... 111

## CHAPTER II.

Macullah first visited—its appearance from Seaward—its Houses—Amount of Population—Commerce—Somarelies—Banians—their love of gain—Attachment to and care of Bullocks—Slaves in Arabia—Expedition to enter Africans as Seamen—Visit Shaher—its Governor, Ali Ney—Ceremonies at the Feast of the Aids—Theft, how punished—Succession to the Government ... ... ... ... 137

## CHAPTER III.

Page

Approach Cape Aden—Strength of Fortifications—Jews—Author proceeds to Lahesdj—Caravan Assemblies—Docility and Fleetness of Camels—Arrives at the Sultan's Palace—Bedowins attack the City—Appearance of the Coast between Aden and Shaher. Natural Divisions of Arabia—Jaffa and Hydramaut—North-east Monsoon, its duration and influence—Erroneous position assigned to the Bay of Hargiah—Islands off the Coast—Tides ... ... ... ... 156

## CHAPTER IV.

Arrive at Socotra—Its appearance—Contradictory descriptions—Tamarida—its Houses—Cemeteries—Suspicion of its Inhabitants—Quit the Town—Perilous Pass—Camels—Cadhoop—Caverns serving as Habitations—Face of the Country—Process of making Knives—Tanning Skins—Inscriptions—Resemblance to the early Ethiopic—A Steamer passes—Socotran Marriage—Amusements—Slaves ... 178

## CHAPTER V.

Noxious Insects—Storm—Singular Caverns—Devastation of Torrents—Nebek Trees—Reservoir of Rain Water—Singular Trees—Visited by the Mountaineers—their Voracity—ascend the Mountains—deep and fertile Ravines—enter a Cave—Female astonishment—Presents — Invitation — Singular Habitations—Scene at Night—Physical appearance of Mountaineers—Golenseah—its indifferent Water—Quit

Page

Golenseah and again ascend the Mountains—Want of Water—Aloes—Civet Cats—Goats ... ... ... 201

## CHAPTER VI.

Discharge our Guide—Furious Storm—Rough Treatment of a Camel—Beauty of the Scenery of Socotra—Fears of the Inhabitants—Date Groves—Attempt to reach the Summit of the Mountains—Unexpected Opposition—Quarrel—Sunday—Feast of the Ramadan—Quit the Town—Itinerant Merchant—Female Curiosity—Abundance of Water—Mode of milking Goats—Visit the Granite Mountains... ... ... 229

## CHAPTER VII.

Ascend the Granite Mountains — Snake — Romantic Scenery—General Configuration of the Range—Mortality of Troops—Singular Mode of Interment—Ancient Custom ... ... ... ... ... ... 264

## CHAPTER VIII.

Form and Geographical Features—Climate—Productions—Dragon's Blood—Natural History—Government—Language—Diseases—Peculiar Customs—Religion—Former and present State of the Island continued ... ... ... ... ... ... ... 281

## CHAPTER IX.

Occupation of Men and Women—Process of Ignition—Bedowin Cheerfulness—Modes of Salutation—

Page

Language—Numerals—Diseases—Traditions—Mixed Population—Religion—Island, how peopled—Conclusion ... ... ... ... ... ... 310

Appendix ... ... ... ... ... ... 334

# MESOPOTAMIA,

AND THE

# SHORES OF THE MEDITERRANEAN.

## CHAPTER I.

Arrive at Tripoli—Author falls in love—Customs of various Countries—Quit Tripoli—Reflections.

I AGAIN found myself at Tripoli. Secluded as I had been for many months from the civilized world, the society of two young and beautiful girls, daughters of mine host, communicated a charm which for a time averted or absorbed all other pursuits; and, without a care or a thought, I gave myself wholly up to the fascination and delight I derived from their companionship. Trite and true is the remark, that obstacles but whet our inclinations to the attainment of our wishes. In Europe our intercourse with the softer sex is less reserved than in the East; yet here, when females do appear, a modest and gentle demeanour marks their deportment, and compensates in a great measure for their absence at other periods. No affectation of reserve or coyness, no flutter or bustle, can then be traced; they move and act as if discharging a natural duty. And must I avow it, myself, a traveller of the world, without for an instant wishing to detract from the merits of my own countrywomen, I am, as regards mere general intercourse, as well pleased with the manners of the one as the other.

Hypatia, the eldest, had barely reached the dawn of Oriental womanhood—she had seen but sixteen summers; yet conception never originated, nor chisel wrought, a more lovely being. Of a stature the tallest consistent with female beauty, her limbs were rounded and of exquisite symmetry; her feet and hands, after the fashion of her country, were left uncovered, the nails of either being tinged with henna, and equal care bestowed on both, which were femininely small; the blue veins which intersected them denoted the Georgian blood by which they were traversed. Her features possessed eminently the characteristics of her race—they were truly Greek. Her hair, dark, rich, and flowing, when unconfined fell as low as her waist; her eyes were large, soft, and speaking, with eye-lashes of yet a deeper tinge than black is usually considered; throwing a fringed shadow over a cheek of almost transparent delicacy, yet warmed by a sunny hue that would clear it from the charge of *insipidity*. Her forehead, of marble paleness, was crossed by eyebrows, arched, but barely a line in breadth; they met over a nose slightly aquiline, but shadowing an upper lip, thin, but projecting over the pouting prettiness of the lower. Was it a *moustache*, whose light yet glossy tinge fringed the former?

In countries with a mixed population, having blacks on the one hand and a fair race on the other, it seems invariably the custom that their inhabitants estimate ideas of beauty, and otherwise demean themselves, to assimilate their persons as much to the fairer as possible; it is only when little or no communication with whites has been held, as in central Africa, that they are looked on with disgust and abhorrence. The practice of staining the hands and feet with henna, (which, like most other Oriental usages, is alluded to in the earliest pages of the Scriptural narrative,) would appear to have owed its origin to this motive. The skin, and especially the extremities, of those who people the torrid regions, or the countries bordering on them, is far colder than that of Europeans; and their nails are therefore of a leaden or bluish colour, similar to what an European's would be when affected by cold. In order to bring about the roseate hue which tinges those of the latter when in health, Orientals have recourse to henna. When first plastered on, it has a very unsightly appearance, and two or three days are sufficient to wear it from their hands and feet; but the nails retain an almost crimson tint for several weeks. When the hair is to be coloured, it is first plastered over with a preparation of indigo; this after a few hours is removed, henna applied, and after that being washed off, the hair is found to be of a glossy blackness. The latter process is more practised by the men than the women. Such with my two Greek fair ones would have been as needless as to "gild refined gold or paint the lily."

The other sister, Anna, I will not attempt to describe—she was

> "Somewhat fat, and languishing, and lazy;
> But of a beauty which would drive you crazy."

Good-nature, affability, and meekness, were blended in their characters, and marked the appearance and deportment of both; but the elder, with a slight degree more of reserve, might be said to personify those qualities which the younger, light of heart, put in practice.

How varied are human customs, though none perhaps more so than those which regard the general estimate of feminine delicacy. An Arab, Persian, or Egyptian female, surprised in a state of nudity, seeks only at the moment to conceal her face. Throughout the Burmese empire, the females walk forth with a wrapper wholly open in the front, and exposing at each step nearly the whole of the lower part of their persons. On the coast of Malabar, the virtuous female exposes her bosom, while those of looser deportment wholly conceal theirs. European ideas appear in general little opposed to the low dresses of the modern ball-room, or of witnessing the agile feats of an opera dancer; while the Levantine females, whose dress other wise carefully envelopes all the rest of the person, even to their feet, exposes the whole of the bosom, which is retained only by an almost imperceptible net-work. But it would wholly violate Turkish and Grecian ideas of propriety to do so, and the dress in consequence fits tightly round their necks, and entirely conceals them. Otherwise, their costume is superb; consisting of a profusion of gay colours, but well disposed. The head is decked with diamonds and pearls, the hair being plaited and falling in rich profusion to the waist, where it is braided and fastened by gold knots.

My accent and knowledge of European customs soon gained that credence which my appearance and Moslem garb, notwithstanding repeated declarations to that effect, had not at first obtained for me, *viz.* that I was an Englishman and Christian; and, as I have before mentioned, in the course of a few days I found myself completely domesticated with the family. Be it remembered, that it is of Greeks I am speaking, where, in contradiction to Mahomedan usages and customs, both sexes in a family mix freely with each other. Our almost first object was to select a small corner in the divan, which, for want of a better, answered as a boudoir. In the centre of our spacious apartment there was a marble fountain, the falling waters of which either lulled us to repose, or amused us with its murmurs. All the furniture in the room consisted of the divan, covered with the richest cloth, its cushions of blue velvet; and costly carpets were spread over the marble floor.

Here, when I was within the house, I passed a most delightful time, either in playing chess, chatting in Turkish, or smoking. Let not the too sensitive European take alarm at the latter amusement, unladylike as it may appear; for the Syrian tobacco used here is highly aromatic, and has nothing in its fumes noxious or offensive. There is as much elegance of attitude displayed, while holding the chebouque, and seated on a Persian carpet, as perhaps in the finest form of an European bending over her harp, or moving in the mystic circle of the waltz. Our divan was pillowed with the softest cushions. About every half-hour coffee and a fresh chebouque were brought in by my fair attendant. Etiquette required, as I received the golden cup, or the mouth of the pipe, from her fair soft hand, that I should slightly bow my head, which was returned on her part by a gentle inclination of the body, placing at the same time the hand on the heart.

When the glorious orb of light hid its beams beneath the mountainous masses of Lebanon, and the work of the day was concluded, we used to dine in a small alcove in the garden. The meal was always prepared by a slave, under the direction of the two sisters. Whatever may be the condition of a female in the East, however high in station, she conceives it no derogation of her dignity to superintend the minutest trifles of the household affairs; and this in nowise detracts from their gentle and feminine demeanour. An European female, who engages much in domestic drudgery, it may be observed, can scarcely fail to lose in a measure these qualities. They never, however, partook of our meal; but stood during the repast behind us, with small porous jars of water in their hands, which, with some favourite dish, they smilingly pressed on our notice. Our dinner rarely occupied more than ten minutes; for an Asiatic eats to live—an European lives to eat. Here there were neither chairs, tables, knives, forks, nor plates; one dish, common to all, appears at a time, though twenty may be brought in succession. When it was concluded, and the ladies and female servants had made their repast, the eternal pipes and coffee, with the occasional conversation of some looker-in, finished the evening, and about eleven we retired for the night.

A life so listless and inactive may appear scarcely compatible with that of bustling activity, and beset with so many adventures and perils as mine which preceded it had been; but man, if not a creature of circumstances, is certainly a creature of climate. In travelling, we pluck of the tree of knowledge; our eyes are opened, the rough angles of early prejudice are worn off, and we are taught to compare and generalize. What, for instance, is more common than to hear a scampering tourist railing against the sensuality of Turks for indulging in such luxuries as I have described? Yet those who practise them will start from their harem to the war-horse, and remain in the saddle for several days. Such men, be it remembered, but a century ago, encamped beneath the walls of Vienna. Reverse the picture: conduct a Turk to England—he who in his own country reposes in lofty halls, or even in the open air—take him to the confined air of an European bed-room, and point out an European sweltering under a heap of bed-clothes—would any other feeling than that of unqualified disgust arise in his mind?

Could it happen otherwise, associated as I was day by day with these girls, than that I should fall in love? I did so. My affections, however, long wavered between the two; a slight incident eventually turned the scale. Unknown to them I had followed the two sisters to the bazaar, to which they were journeying, after the heat of the day, to purchase some sweetmeats for our coming meal. This is the most busy part of the day, and the streets were crowded. As they were passing a coffee-shop, out started an opium-eating fanatic, who, from seeing a Greek servant with them, deemed them to be of that persuasion, and therefore fit objects for insult. Accordingly he placed himself before the ass on which Anna was mounted, and refused to allow it to proceed. In the bustle some persons behind unconsciously urged the beast forward, when the ruffian drew his yataghan, and was about to cut the poor animal over the head, but I sprung forward, and with one blow of my sheathed sabre brought him to the ground. He rose and dashed at me with all the fury of a maniac, but my weapon was drawn and his life in my power; unwilling to slay him, I directed my blow to his right arm, which fell powerless by his side.

What has taken me some time to describe was but the work of a few seconds. The spectators, startled by the suddenness of the affair, had hitherto looked on without interference; but they now rushed upon, disarmed, and bore him cursing and shouting from the spot. Never supposing me otherwise than what I appeared to be, a Mahomedan, my conduct in defending a female thus publicly insulted, drew upon me the congratulations and plaudits of every one. Had my real creed been known, this interference might have been differently estimated. This is the only time, in an Eastern city, I have known a female to be treated otherwise than with respect in the streets; every one there makes way for them, be their rank what it may.

When our party met at dinner, the fracas of course was introduced, and the elder sister thanked me repeatedly for the part I had taken. The younger spoke not during the evening; her eyes, however, led me to hope she was not the less grateful; and when I took her soft hand within my own to wish her good night, the touch thrilled through me—she did not reject the gentle pressure I gave it. That night Anna's name was mingled with prayers, and my rest was feverish and broken.

On the following morning I arose with a determination to learn how far I had reason to hope or despair. Strolling forth into the garden, I found the father seated beneath an alcove, smoking his pipe. He motioned me to be seated, and with a smile inquired the subject which had caused me to assume a more than usual seriousness? My affair was soon settled. An Englishman, in pay from Government, I offered to marry his daughter. The old man removed his pipe, and coolly remarked—"Friend, you came into my family a stranger, and in the garb of a Moslem; no inquiries did I or they make respecting either your country or faith; much pleasure have I and they derived from your society, and still more should we, did you but remain amidst us; but the daughters of my house have hitherto wed but with those of their own country and their own faith; for the present, therefore, seek no close alliance with us. Such, however, is the personal regard which I entertain for you, that, provided you will engage in my business, aid me with advice and assistance, and remain in the same mind twelve months hence, my daughter shall be thine." Thus concluded the longest speech the father had probably ever made. As he called for another pipe, I briefly thanked him, and after performing my morning ablutions, I joined the ladies, whom I found seated at breakfast. Their eyes must have "told a flattering tale;" for, as we indulged with innocent badinage, respecting some peculiarities of the father, they sparkled and beamed with delight.

The power which the human being possesses of commanding all animated nature, seems to depend upon the effect of vision. With respect to reason, as it is called, I doubt if many brutes do not possess a larger share than falls to the lot of many of our own kind. With the eye we command the maniac. No animal, Sir Walter Scott remarks, but will quail before the glance of a desperate and wholly reckless man. View the same agent operating with a person excited by any of those thousand-and-one passions which agitate and swell the human breast, and mark its effects on his listeners—the glistening eye, the dilated and then expanded pupil—and we at once arrive at a conclusion, from our present knowledge of anatomy, which the ancients were ignorant of, that the brow is the seat of reason, although the connection between the eye and the brain must ever remain a mystery.

I pass over, as not of any particular interest, the few weeks which followed my assumption of a mercantile pursuit. The period was one of no satisfaction to me, for I found, notwithstanding my boasted readiness to shift my character, that the craft entailed such chicanery—such "lying, slandering, and all uncharitableness"—that even I stood aghast, as the old man one day pressed me to sell a parcel of old clothes belonging to some Jews who the year before had died of the plague; and for a time, despite of Anna's love, beauty, gold, and commercial fame, determined to mend my ways.

Accordingly, unknown to all, I purchased a small skiff, eighteen feet in length, six in breadth, and provided with sail and oars.

I am apt, as my readers know, to digress now and then; and I beg them to excuse my doing so once more (I do not promise it shall be the last time), on a point of some importance, which has been recalled to my thoughts by the recent death of a friend from cholera.

Sir Isaac Newton, it is said, was induced to consider the laws of gravitation from seeing an apple fall from a tree; and by watching the minute operations of nature, we not unfrequently arrive in a similar manner at a knowledge of the general laws by which they are regulated. A few days before I penned these lines, nervous excitement, brought on by intense study and application to such a variety of subjects that time was scarcely left me to eat, drink, or sleep, induced me, for quietude, to take a cottage at a watering-place not far from London. It had not been occupied for twelve months; the season was very rainy, the grounds in its vicinity saturated, the drains stopped; and first one, then another, of those sent to clean the house were attacked with cholera symptoms. By adopting an Indian mode of treatment, brandy and laudanum, they were cured. Notwithstanding the prognostications of those in the neighbourhood, that it would be impossible to cause water to flow to a higher elevation than the stream, by constructing embankments and mimic locks, I compelled it to do so, and drained the cottage. Perhaps it is necessary I should state that the patch of ground on which this was situated was intersected by drains in every direction, and I now procured, from the percolation of the water around, a clear running stream. One morning, as I strolled along the bank of the ditch which conveys the water from the premises, I was induced to consider the motion of the stream actuated by the wind which swept by and along the banks—it progressed in circles. I thought of the recent discoveries in the laws of storms of Colonel Reed, and his hurricanes. Suddenly it occurred to me that the atmosphere receives its impetus and direction from the flow of the ocean of rivers and water in general; and hence I deem it not impossible, that the mysterious manner in which this fearful disorder, cholera, marched its eccentric and awful course might be traced, and the apparent incongruity of its sweeping one side of a street and leaving the other scathless accounted for.

The human mind can never conceive a beginning or end. Diseases must have a beginning, but who can trace them out. Cholera, under that name, first, I believe, broke out in the

Marquis of Hastings' army; but it had, under the name of *mort de chien*, been previously known to the Portuguese. Hence it took the directions of the principal river, and became otherwise distributed by atmospheric currents over the face of the country. Be that as it may, it would appear to have its origin in want of cleanliness and free ventilation; and I conclude this chapter with the remark, that for the future, in England, we need not fear that this scourge can make any progress, provided on its first appearance measures to effect these objects are forthwith taken.

## CHAPTER II.

Engage a Servant—Sail for Cyprus—Tyre—Cushites—Himyaritic Writing identical with the Language of Job—Still a spoken Language—Queen Sheba—Concluding Remarks.

BIDDING my friends adieu, I one morning made my way down to the beach, where I discovered a boy, who had cast his net, and caught nothing. I looked at him for an instant—he returned my glance.

"Who are you?"

"A Maltese—my name is Jim. I am a fisherman."

"Good Jim, my fortunes at present are not very bright; will you leave your fishing, and follow me?"

"Willingly," replied Jim, who spoke in Arabic; "I feel I shall like you." He was about to leave his net behind—

"Not so," said I, "that may prove of service."

We sought our boat. I had previously purchased a small skin of wine, and this we finished after we had launched our boat, and named her the "Nancy."

Still I was not at ease. The affection which I had formed for the beauteous Anna might be seared over with the hot iron of impatience, but there was the healthy matter beneath, requiring but the removal of the superficial to bring it forth.

For three days did I strive to persuade the charming Anna to quit the paternal roof, and become the companion of my wanderings; but all in vain; the crafty Greek was a Greek, and a female—what chance had I? In vain I serenaded; in vain I spoke of other fairer lands. She would walk—would talk, not prattle—as long as I pleased within the walls of her father's grounds, but no persuasion could draw her beyond them. I was eager and willing, before God and man, to call her mine; but where—where was the bridal feast to appear—the bridal virgins—their lamps, their gay attire, their gorgeous room, their fatted calf?

I was in despair. "Jim," said I, "let us turn fishermen."

In pursuance of this scheme, we quitted the harbour, but fortunately saw nothing until we arrived at Larmica, a port in the island of Cyprus. Greatly were the Turks astonished at our venturing in so small a craft where we had. They had nothing but biscuits, which they very freely gave to us.

Returning to the coast, I saw my love once more; was again disappointed in inducing her to leave, and again took my departure for Tyre.

As the winter was now approaching, we were obliged to hasten to the northern ports of the Mediterranean, as they are then unapproachable.

The present Tyre, however, furnishes us with little to denote the city of the waves. Strange it is—widely spread as was the empire of the Phœnicians, widely extended as was their commerce, vast their resources—so few monuments should of all these have remained. Their very language may be said to have passed away; for can the few words preserved by Plautus be depended on as genuine?

Their inscriptions are yet more doubtful; while the monuments which remain only leave the subject in greater obscurity. The latter possess, however, the highest and most prominent claims on our interest; and the labours of such men as Gesenius may yet enable us to decipher that which led to the infant efforts of commerce, the migration of nations, the progress of the various languages which now are spoken by the varied human race, and finally lay open the hitherto mist-enveloped pages of early profane history. There are those who cry to all new—*cui bono*? Let them apply that question to themselves.

It has been put forth that the language of the Maltese is a relic of that of the Phœnician. The position is plausible: the Phœnicians were the earliest navigators by the way of the Red Sea; they were in constant intercourse with the Arabs, and doubtless acquired, if it was not their original, the Arabic language, to facilitate commercial intercourse with that people. The Arabic I believe to be the oldest language in the world; the Hebrew being a collateral branch of it. The Maltese speak a corrupt Arabic, and hence I conclude their's may be a relic of the Phœnician. Indeed, the learned, with few exceptions, allow that the Phœnician language was identical with the Hebrew.

Montfaucon first made the lucky guess that the legend on the Sidonian coins must be read לצר. In 1735, a trilingual inscription was found at Malta; another, in 1745, was discovered in Cyprus by Dr. Pococke, and described by him.

The question has been asked, Who were the Phœnicians? That we shall probably discover with the decipherment of their language.

Impressed with such thoughts, I wandered over the fallen ruins of Tyre: I called to mind

Alexander's attack, his final success, and the cruelties which marked it; that those who formerly dwelt amidst columns and palaces, where now camels are browsing, might perchance have visited my own green isle; that we have even, if Valency and Sir William Betham's testimony be accredited, even in ancient and modern Erse (if the latter be not a bull), preserved their language. "It shall be a rock, on which fishers shall cast and dry their nets."

Some months ago Lieut. Wellsted forwarded to the Royal Geographical Society of London *fac-similes* of certain inscriptions found by him at Nukub-el-Hedjer, on the south coast of Arabia; and in a subsequent communication to the Royal Asiatic Society, more recently published, he adds some remarks which suggested themselves to him, as to their origin and purport. As they are intimately blended with the preceding remarks, they are here transcribed:—

"At the period of the promulgation of the Koran two alphabets were used in Arabia—the Kufic, in which that work is written; and which we are still able to decipher, and the Himyaritic, adopted by the people of Yemen, but which, until I found it, was supposed to be lost to us. I know not, therefore, on what grounds certain philologists have conjectured it bore a strong affinity to the Ethiopic; but, when the Koran appeared in the Kufic character, the inhabitants of Yemen were unable to read it. Ludolfus says, Ethiopic is derived immediately from the Arabic, and that there is so perfect an agreement between them, that he who understands the one will understand the other. Ludolfus passed sixty years in acquiring a knowledge of the former of these languages, and the fact of the identity he mentions, may aid us with the inscriptions. According to Eusebius, about the time the Israelites were in Egypt, a body of Arabs, the early descendants from Cush, crossed the straits of Bab-el-mandeb, and passed into Ethiopia; and most of the Asiatic nations, at the time of Josephus, considered these two classes as of common origin. The Cushites invented the alphabet, says Ludolfus, which he gives in his work, and which he believes to be older than the Kufic. According to Strabo, the Auasis, or Abases, were fertile spots in the desert. A tribe took their name from these, and, it is said, crossed over the Red Sea; and from these Abases, as they were called, Abyssinia received its modern appellation.

"Sir William Jones, in his annual address,

more than once alludes to this desideratum; and, in a Memoir addressed by the French academicians to the King of Denmark, seventy-five years ago, it formed one of Michaelis' questions (p. 247) for the solution of the celebrated Danish travellers, who were about to proceed to Yemen. Michaelis appears to have been fully aware of the importance of obtaining this character and language.

"It has frequently been a subject of regret that we were in possession of no inscriptions from the country, by which these points might be determined. Niebuhr, during his stay in Arabia, sought in vain for them. (Vol. i. pp. 484, 485.) I add, that, owing to the locality in which these inscriptions are found, and for other reasons, I venture to suggest that these, together with those we found at Hassan Gorab, are in the lost Himyaritic writing. Should this prove the case, the resemblance to the Ethiopic is not conjectural, since a complete identity in many of the letters can be traced.

"My knowledge of Oriental literature is so scanty, having been from my boyhood actively engaged in my professional pursuits, that I offered these remarks with much diffidence. They have, however, received an unexpected confirmation, by the publication of a learned paper by M. Roediger,* and by the labours of the profound Gesenius, who, from those I copied from the ruins of Nukub-el-Hedjer, has even succeeded in deciphering the words 'King of the Himyarites.' On this subject, the Geographical Society (vol. viii. p. 265), in a review of the Ethnography of the African races, observes —'Dr. Pritchard brings arguments to prove that the Abyssinian alphabet was derived from the Himyarites, and not invented by the first Christian missionaries at Axum, as Michaelis and other biblical writers have supposed; and here we may observe, that it has been discovered by Lieutenant Wellsted that such was precisely the fact. The letters of the Abyssinians, or characters nearly resembling them, have been used of old by the Himyarites; and this discovery, anticipated from a survey of historic probabilities made by a British naval officer, has put an end to a controversy long agitated amongst the European literati, as to the era and manner in which the Abyssinians came to be possessed of the art of writing.'

"Let me now draw the attention of the Society to a few facts, which, if followed up with diligence and interest, may perhaps lead to yet

* Zeitschrift der Kunde des Morgenlandes.—Goett. 1837, 8vo. p. 322.

more important discoveries. The Himyaritic characters represented one of the leading and distinct dialects of Arabia; and their grammarians tell a story of an Arab of Hedjaz, who, being directed by a King of the Himyarites to sit down, threw himself over a precipice, because the word *theb*, instead of sit down, signifies, in the Koraish dialect, leap down. Now, before we can hope for any facility, or even any degree of certainty in deciphering these inscriptions, we must possess ourselves of this dialect. Singular, therefore, is it that Edrisi * should tell us, 'that the people of Mahrah † speak a very corrupt language—it is,' says he, 'the ancient Himyaritic.' Indeed nothing is more likely than that it should be so, for, since the time of Mahomed, there is reason to believe both Mahrah and Hydramaut have never known a master, and that therefore they should have retained their ancient language.

"During my stay in Arabia, I procured a few words of the dialect; but, not knowing their importance, I did not care to collect more; nor was I until very recently made aware that we

* Translation of Edrisi. Paris edition, 1836, p. 150.

† Mahrah is a very ancient name of a province on the S. E. coast of Arabia, and joining to Hydramaut; spelt Nazaramath in the Bible.

had any specimens of it in Europe, since no traveller had, to my knowledge, visited Mahrah. But the Rev. G. C. Renouard, Honorary Foreign Secretary to the Royal Geographical Society, tells me that the language is a cognate dialect of the Arabic, and that my vocabulary is probably similar to that of which a specimen is preserved by M. Fresnell, in one of the last numbers of the 'Journal Asiatique.' I now give a few words, which Mr. Renouard has kindly translated for me. The words were, at the time they were collected by me, also written in Persian, and hence we have been enabled to explain them in English:—

"*M'hárah* Tongue.—Rúrú*, sea; *kirmím*, mountain; *rabugh*, sweet water; *híríz*, rice; *sayyid*, fish; *khobz*, bread; *'afrút, jawárí,—i. e.* millet, sorghum vulgare (I believe); *bilnít*, white jawárí; *bikríd*, ox; *tibuwít*, goat; *khúf*, lion; *ghíkk*, man; *hirmít*, woman; *hibríz*, grandfather; *hír*, an ass; *dik*, a cock; *dikiwik*, a bird; *rehbeït*, a town; *sáyit*, a she mule; *chibár*, a giant; *heïbít*, a camel; *therniz*, a leopard; *mankhalít*, a palm; *limít*, a lemon; *lím*, a pomegranate;

* Probably a Hindú misspelling, on the part of the Persian who wrote these words, for Mahrah, since the Arabs have no aspirated letters—b'h, t'h, d'h, like the Hindús, or m'h, like the Mahrattas.

*khitab*, wood; *mah*, oil; *herzúb*, lead; *rí*, marrow; *sheprah*, a lip; *dek-hen*, beard; *elbeden*, or *elíden*, a tooth; *hest*, hand; *sháff*, hair; *khít*, city.

"Much as my will would lead me, my ability is not equal to following this subject up in all its bearings; and I therefore for the present must content myself with putting forth a few hints, which may serve those who can.

"M. Fresnell has quoted an Arabian proverb, indicative that he who would go to Zhafar (or Jaffa), adjoining to Hydramaut, must speak the Himyaritic dialect; and broadly states the fact of its being still a spoken language—having indeed, at Jiddah, a servant from thence, whose native language it is: he gives a few words, and, in the inflection of a verb, without himself being probably aware of it, M. Fresnell has proved the strong affinity of the Himyaritic to the Ethiopic. But, to place the matter beyond doubt, let us forthwith obtain a copious vocabulary from Arabia. Any one of the Company's vessels of war, on her way between India and Egypt, can touch at Kisseen, where men will be found speaking the Mahrah language.

"Very little is known in Europe respecting the Himyaritic empire; but the Arabian historians say that the greater part of Arabia Felix, comprehending Yemen, Saba, and Hydramaut, were governed by princes of the tribe of Himyar, who bore the general title and surname of Tobba.* This kingdom is said to have lasted two thousand years, to have extended its limits to India, and to have numbered amidst its monarchs the celebrated Queen Sheba. According to Abulfeda, it existed two thousand and twenty years, or above three thousand, if we believe Ahmed Ibn Yusuf and El Janaubus. The history of the Kings of Himyar, or the 'Great Kings,' as they were styled, has been written by Shahabbedin Ahmed Ibn Abdelvahab, Al Bekri, Al Teimi, Al Kendi, surnamed Nouari, author of an universal history, which he dedicated to Nassa Mahomed Ibn Kalaoun, Sultan of the Mamalukes. For an account of this work *vide* D'Herbelot. A series of these kings is given from Joctan to the times of Mahomed. Diodorus tells us that Arabia Felix, or at least that part of it called Sabea, was so immensely rich, that all the wealth of the world seemed to centre there. Gold was found in large lumps, and was so plentiful that all their furniture was made of it. Agatharchides bears

* Signifying successor; assumed in the same manner as Cæsar by the Romans Emperors, and Caliph by the successors of the Prophet.

the same glowing testimony to the wealth and luxury of the Sabeans. Although the annals of the Himyarite dynasty are doubtless blended with fable, yet there seems good reason to believe that some of the Arabian monarchs were both enterprising and powerful.

"Abu Kurrub Tobba,* it is said, led an army into Chinese Tartary, and on his way there left twelve thousand Arabs as a body of reserve to retire upon, in case of discomfiture; he succeeded in this remote and perilous expedition, and after an absence of seven years led his army back with immense spoil in safety to Yemen. There is reason to believe this is not the extravagant fiction it at first sight appears; for the twelve thousand Arabs were never withdrawn, and vestiges of the race are still said to exist in different parts of Turkistan; but what is deserving equal attention is, that on the early conquest of Bokhara by the Mahomedans, an inscription was found over one of its gates expressly recording the presence of Tobba the Himyarite. If this was the case, it would be in the same character as that which I found at Nukub-el-Hedjer; indeed I believe some of the Arabian historians state the fact, that it was in the Himyaritic character, and if preserved by

* "The Father of Affliction."

any of these writers, will at once be decisive both of this historical question and the nature (should there yet be doubt) of that character.* Let me here observe, that as an Ethiopian dynasty, a short time before the time of Mahomed, for seventy-two years filled the throne of Yemen, it may be anticipated that some of the inscriptions brought from thence will be the characters then used by that people; such, indeed, are perhaps those found at Hassan Gorab, differing in some respects from those at Nukub-el-Hedjer. A *fac-simile* of both is appended to this paper, together with others of those found at Sa'na and in Yucutan.

"A resemblance† between my inscription at Nukub-el-Hedjer and that on the Lāt of Feraz Shah, at Delhi, has also been conjectured, but apparently without foundation; but one has indeed been found on the pedestal of a small statue, and deposited in the Museum of the Asiatic Society of Bombay; and other inscriptions in Central Asia should be diligently sought for. At first sight, a striking resemblance may be traced between the Himyari characters and those on the ancient Bactrian coins deciphered

* I am indebted to Major Price's Essay towards the History of Arabia, p. 98, for these details.

† Geographical Journal.

by Mr. Prinsep in the Calcutta Asiatic Journal, and it is possible a further examination may prove their identity. If so, the happy conjectures of Dr. Leipsius, in his tract on Indian Palæography, will receive an unexpected confirmation.

"There can be little doubt but that this character and language is one of the oldest (if not the oldest) on the face of the globe. 'Writing was known to Job and to the Himyarites many centuries before Mahomed, as appears from some ancient monuments said to remain in that character.'* One of these 'ancient monuments,' therefore, it has been my good fortune to discover. Again, the same authority† says, 'The Himyarites were not strangers to the art of writing; the characters used by them were the most ancient of any used by the Arabs; from the mutual dependence of the letters or parts upon each other, it was called El Mosnad.' Those who wish to pursue this subject of the Himyaritic character can consult Ab-Farauzabadus, Ibn Athir, Abulfeda, El Jarma, El Khalim, and Georgius Ibn Hamed. At this point, however, we have enough to pronounce that a new Semetic language is probably before us, which may, in ancient times, have extended

* Universal History, vol. xvi. p. 283. † Ibid. p. 284.

over Asia, and which by future researches promises to add a new Bible to the collection of our Polyglots. I do not hesitate even to predict that we have enough before us to shake, in a measure, the belief in a portion of our present system of comparative geography; for example, I will give a few points which at the moment suggest themselves to me. The Israelites, in their wanderings, are declared to have reached the land of Edom, which our geographers, on Greek authority, place in Arabia Petrea. Now, in the course of a few days, I shall be enabled to show the Society that there are two dialects of the Arabian language, of which we have hitherto been profoundly ignorant—one, that of Marah, the ancient Himyaritic; and the other, the Ehkilli, spoken by the people of Kisseen and Socotra, so nearly resembling it, that the people of one country can understand those of the other. In a copious vocabulary which I have given of the latter language in the Geographical Society's Journal, the word 'Ophir' occurs, meaning 'red;' now Himyar, the name of this ancient empire, means also 'red;' hence I hope to prove the frequent recurrence of the word 'red' in early times—the Red Land, the Red Sea; or, as I should render it, the land of Edom, the Sea of Edom. Solomon's fleets then took their departure from the ports of Elath and Esiangeber, situated, as is expressly mentioned, 'at the head of the Red Sea,'* and visited the ports of Ophir, South Arabia, Tarshish, and those of Africa, where all the products, apes, peacocks, gold, &c. enumerated in the scriptural narrative, would be found. With respect to the period consumed in this voyage, considering the stormy nature of the Red Sea, and that they had to creep in-shore amidst the reefs, watch the monsoons, &c. &c., the time specified is not too long.

"A word more on the subject of names, in respect of the Queen of Sheba's visit. I must think we have hitherto paid but too little attention to Arabian names and Arabian tradition. It is true the latter are much blended with fable; but, notwithstanding this, let it be remembered that it was here most of the events recorded in Holy Writ were transacted, and that Arabia is moreover a country which, in customs, in language, &c., has changed less than any other. As yet, too, we have but penetrated its confines; the whole of the interior remains unknown to us. Before I made my

* The words "in the land of Edom," which follow, I take to be merely indicative that the whole of Arabia might occasionally be called Edom, from its richest province, or from the ports bordering on the Sea of Edom.

journey into Hydramaut, no European had visited it; and our geographers, despite Greek and Arabian authors, and truth, have marked the whole country as a desert. Let us not, therefore, so hastily reject Arabian authority.

"Do not, in reply to this, urge, that before the time of Mahomed the Arabians had no literature, and that all anterior to this era was borrowed from the Hebrew writings. I very much doubt the fact; and as regards the affinity of names, let any one take up the Bible, and trace in that volume those preserved in the Arabian authors, and those which still exist, and have existed from all time. I will give, which is enough for my present purpose, two identifications of ancient names with those of this country at present retained—Nazarameth, Hydramaut, and Sheba Saba, or Marab. That the latter was Belkis, or the Queen of Sheba's country, I have not the slightest doubt;* the natives of Sa'na state their belief that it is so; and there was no great effort in her journeying by land from Saba to Jerusalem, a distance of about twelve hundred miles: she would then come from a far country, and what is equally

* In Myles Cavendish's Translation of the Bible, 1 Kings, x., it is positively rendered "Queen of rich Arabia." Tindal's, still more corroborative, has it "Queen of Saba."

strange and corroborative of this, she would also come from Yemen—'the South.'

"Now, as there are the strongest reasons to believe the Himyarites, or old Arabs, were the earliest traders in the communication between the eastern and western world, the Arabian Gulf, and even the whole of the Indian Ocean, would, by the early Greek geographers, be styled Erythras, or Red, from the people who traded on its waters; and we thus gain an easy solution of that on which volumes of controversial learning have been expended.

"Again, without any far-fetched theory, is not Himyar the land of Edom? Are all those marchings and counter-marchings, so minutely described in the Bible, to be confined to Arabia Petrea, in which our geographers, to secure Edom its present condition, have placed them? Is it not more than probable that people extended their wanderings over the whole peninsula, and reached its southern confines of Yemen, or Himyar, or Edom? The old Hebrew and the Arabian names of places on their route would differ but little from each other; nor would the modern Arabian differ so much as is usually supposed. Without being aware of any of these facts, a learned Jewish Rabbin told us that he was perfectly astounded, on his way up the Red Sea, to find so many *Hebrew* names retained there. Those who are qualified can easily follow the path which I have pointed out. Let them seek for ancient and modern maps of Arabia, and endeavour to find the identification we may hope for.

"Now for a few further hints, growing out of this subject, which may lead to the elucidation of two other questions, which have caused equal, if not more discussion—the visit of Solomon's fleet to Tarshish and Ophir, and the congratulatory visit of the Queen of Sheba to that monarch. We will first deal with the former.

"For many reasons, I conceive Tarshish, in its largest sense, to mean Africa; how, otherwise, could the Jewish fleet, without going round the Cape, have left Joppa or Jaffa, if we place Tarshish at Java, or in other parts of the East, as all authors have previously done? But if we consider Tarshish as Africa, and that they visited some portion of its shores washed by the Mediterranean, our difficulties cease. Himyar (South Arabia) and Ophir have already in name been identified; let us do so in reality, and the remaining part of the question is set at rest.

"The identification of the Himyarites and

the Ethiopians, which has been alluded to in a former part of this paper, may account for the frequent mention of Queen Belkis, or Sheba, in the annals of the Abyssinian dynasties which are given by Bruce. Some very curious facts will, doubtless, be elicited when the annals of the Himyarite kings, and those of Ethiopia, come to be further compared and examined; but here for the present, in abler hands than mine, must I leave this interesting subject.

"Tradition, or the pages of history, have preserved to us some recollection of the mighty empires of Assyria, of Babylon, or of Egypt, and their imperishable ruins yet endure above all time, and give a colouring of truth to them; yet an impenetrable veil has been thrown over the Himyaritic empire, and even its very existence seems doubted. That the seat of this empire was and is not destitute of large and populous cities, and even of ancient monuments, is made evident by the list I have given of the former,* and by my discovery of the ruins of Nukub-el-Hedjer.* A wall, constructed of blocks of hewn marble, thirty feet in height, and carried round a hill half a mile in circumference, would attract attention in any country; but here, in

* *Vide* Wellsted's Travels in Arabia, vol. ii. p. 446.

connexion with this subject, on a locality our geographers have marked as a desert, it excites the liveliest interest. Intelligence was given me of whole districts which were strewn with similar edifices. The province of Hydramaut abounds in ancient towns; and Marab, or Saba, the capital of the empire, three days' journey to the E. N. E. of Sa'na, is said to have been six miles in circumference. Mr. Cruttenden, of the Indian navy, in a highly interesting narrative, published by the Geographical Society, in the last number of the Journal, informs us that, during his stay at Sa'na, the magnitude of the ruins at Marab was a theme of constant discourse with the Arabs; and he, in the vicinity of Sa'na, found other inscriptions, similar to that which I brought from the latter city. Let us yet hope some officer of the Indian navy, or other branch of the public service, will undertake the investigation of this very interesting portion of the globe; his adventurous spirit will no doubt be amply repaid.

"Almost all the other nations in the world, which were distingushed for their trade and wealth, derived it from hence. From Arabia Felix the ancient Egyptians received their sup-

* *Vide* Wellsted's Travels in Arabia, vol. i. p 426.

plies*—from thence the Tyrians had their richest commodities†—from thence Solomon received such valuable presents‡—and from thence the Egyptians under the Ptolemies received their most valuable merchandize.§ At a later period, from thence the Romans brought all the riches of the East. That most of these articles were from India is doubtless the case; but as there is reason to believe the Arabs brought them, so there is also reason to believe their country would have been enriched by the current of wealth which flowed through it.

"But there is yet one more important fact connected with this subject, which has very recently come to my notice, and to which I beg to solicit the attention of the Society—that since my discovery of the inscriptions of Nukub-el-Hedjer, others have also been discovered in Egypt, in India, and in America; the latter affords abundant matter for speculation. It is to be seen in M. Waldeck's new work on the Province of Yucatan, in South America. This author describes it to have been copied from a collar, found in a cavern, on the neck of an

* Diodorus Siculus, Strabo, Periplus Maris Erythræi.
† Ezekiel, xxxvii.
‡ 1 Kings, 10. 2 Chron. ix.
§ Diodorus Siculus, Dion Cassius, Strabo.

African slave. Was it some ancient amulet, worn by a slave brought recently from Africa? for be it remembered, the character was lost about the time of Mahomed, seven centuries before the supposed discovery of America; or was it carried by some tribe emigrating from Northern Asia to America?

"I fear I have occupied the attention of the Society too long on this subject; but let me advert to the recent appointment of Sir James Carnac, F. R. S., to the governorship of Bombay: he has authorized me to state, that, while there, he will have much pleasure in furthering the views of the Society, on this or any other subject which may have for its object the advancement of science.

"In conclusion, I have only to add, that whither the clue we have thus obtained to the decipherment of these inscriptions will lead, is a point on which I will not permit myself now to speculate; but, if we succeed, it is impossible to conceal that we have in prospect the certainty of deciding on the existence of a mighty empire—one of the oldest languages in the world will be presented in an open volume to us—a light will be thrown on all that space which has hitherto been wrapped in the gloom of ages. The era of letters, the migration of nations, the progress of civilization, the desolating march of eastern conquerors, may be traced; while the traditions and writings of the Arabian and profane authors will not, in this and in other cases, be deemed so wholly unworthy of credence; and, at the same time, we may look forward with confidence to receiving further testimonials to the scrupulous fidelity of the sacred writings."

## CHAPTER III.

Servant's History—Early Miseries—Falls in Love—Visit of his Master—Evasion.

We were now eight miles from Antioch. Leaving Jim in charge of the boat, at daylight I walked to that city. Without any funds at command, I was kindly assisted by the British consul there, to whose hospitality so many travellers have recorded their deep obligations. With a portion of this, and a further sum, which I raised by the sale of my pistols, I purchased an anchor; and, after remaining two days, I rejoined my boat. Fatigue compelled me to remain thus long; and Jim, in the mean time, was left in charge. There was little fear of his starving; although, compelled at length by hunger, he had quitted the boat, and set out for Antioch just as I left it. I waited his return for two days, when we again set sail.

But it is time I gave the reader some further information respecting my companion. A more faithful squire in all my wanderings I had not met with. I have already mentioned that Jim was born at Malta. He had been stolen when young by an American captain, owning a small vessel which traded in sugar and coffee from New York to the Mediterranean. Before he was ten he had crossed the Atlantic. Owing to causes which it will be wholly unnecessary to explain, Jim, whilst the vessel was riding at anchor near New Orleans, escaped from her on board an English schooner. In her he returned to the Mediterranean. Here he served several years in a Sclavonian brig, which was taken by a Greek, and subsequently retaken by a Turkish pirate. He was then sold as a slave at Constantinople; and after living with his master, a Turk, for a year, took offence at the scantiness of his diet, and endeavoured to escape. He was caught, and the usual punishment would have been summarily inflicted, but for the intercession of one of his owner's friends, who had taken a fancy to the lad, and by paying the Turk ten dollars more than that worthy had originally given, Jim found a new and a kinder master.

"Never have I," said he, "since or before, fared so sumptuously as I did then. My master, too, was fond of the forbidden pleasures of wine; and such was his reputation for gallantry, that it was said half the husbands at Pera turned pale whenever he approached that quarter."

"And were you proof," said I, "Jim, against the influence of such an evil example?"

"It becomes not your servant to speak on such matters, although it fell out that I was not; and yet more unfortunately, the object of my attachment was one on whom Zenen Aga had in vain lavished his attentions and his presents. I had been despatched one evening with a budding rose. The fair mistress of the mansion was a widow. Less restraint is imposed by the Mahomedans on that class of females than on any other; it being supposed that their experience as wives, under the tuition of their husbands, had taught them common prudence. Scarcely had I delivered my present into her fair hand, when I was pressed to be seated. In vain I urged the commands of my master for my immediate return. 'She had a message for him'—'some reciprocal token of affection to despatch.'

"With these and other similar excuses she left the apartment, and closed the door without. I heard her clap her hands;* then came the al-

* The Oriental substitute for bells.

most noiseless hurrying of feet, and orders were given for a sumptuous repast to be immediately prepared. Well, thought I, if I am to fall a victim to the Aga's vengeance to-morrow, I may as well *live* to-night: so I composed myself to sleep on a gorgeous crimson velvet divan.

"How long I slept I know not; but I was awakened by feeling two soft and delicate hands pressing my temples. The novelty of my situation, hardly used as I had been from my childhood until I fell into the hands of my present master, had probably in no small degree excited me, and the hostess was alarmed.

The Aga was not rich, and lived fully up to his means; but his dwelling was of an inferior description. I had been reposing, as I have described, on a splendid divan, the cushions of which were strung with lines of pearls. In an open space adjoining there was a fountain playing, the murmur of its waters tending to lull the mind to repose. The morn was shining brightly above, and showed me several lofty citron trees overshadowing the fountain.

"Scarcely had I fully awakened, when the servants entered, bringing with them trays containing all the luxuries which Constantinople could afford. Zuleika, the fair widow, ordered them to be placed on a rich carpet in the centre of the apartment. A slave now approached with an ewer and basin, with which I performed the customary ablutions; for, to outward appearance and customs, I was then a Mahomedan. 'Be seated,' said my fair hostess to me, as she set the example, and plunging her hand into a smoking dish of pilau, she applied herself heartily to a task which I was not slow to follow."

The reader can scarcely fail to be aware that the custom of Mahomedan countries is opposed to the sexes eating with each other. But let Jim continue his narrative.

"You must observe, Khaleil Aga, that my appetite, whenever good fare offers itself, is not bad now; I was younger then, and it was better. I feasted away until repletion compelled me to desist.

"Again my hostess clapped her hands, the slaves appeared, and, upon a sign, every vestige of the feast had disappeared, and the slave, a Nubian, alone remained. Into his hands she delivered a key, which she took from her girdle; another sign, and he also disappeared. A few minutes elapsed, which passed in lively conversation on her part. I replied to her merely in monosyllables. The slave re-entered, bearing with him a silver tray, occupied by the richest wines. 'Try some of that,' said my hostess, addressing me, and pointing to a long bottle, which contained what I have since heard at Malta called champagne; 'that will make you talk.' To my great surprise, she set me the example, by filling and drinking off a large goblet. The bottle was finished between us in a twinkling, and she then had no cause to complain of my silence; for she commenced her tale, and I remained mute during its narration, replenishing my glass whenever a pause in the conversation allowed me to do so.

"She was by birth a Georgian, and had been sold by her parents at the age of fifteen. A wealthy Turk was her purchaser. Fascinated by her charms, he had, previous to setting out on a voyage to Gibraltar, settled all his property on her. Since his departure, now three years, no tidings had been received of him; whether captured by pirates, engulfed in the stormy waters of the Mediterranean, or what other mishap had befallen him, did not yet appear; nor did the fair widow seem much to bemoan his absence, or exhibit much grief for her bereavement."

In thought I anticipated, at this portion of my squire's tale, had the husband, like Sambro, returned and found others feasting on his mutton, how his ire might have been excited. Jim, however, it will appear by the narrative, knew little of such mishaps, and would have perhaps cared less had he known more: but let him continue his tale.

"Hour after hour wiled on in conversation, in joke, and in merriment—when at length we were aroused from midnight summer's dream of pleasure by loud cries at the door. In an instant my hostess was on her feet. She was too well aware of the customs of the police in eastern cities, to be at all apprehensive of our visitors: had any one succeeded in forcing an entrance, she would have concealed me in her harem, which, as its name implies, is sacred from intrusion. The slaves were again summoned, and the Nubian was directed from a window to ascertain what was their object.

"It was my master!

"I was for answering to the well-known tones of his voice. 'Be silent, as you value your life!' interrupted my hostess; 'leave the affair to me.' Approaching the window of the apartment above, she inquired the business of my master.

"'My slave has left me these six hours,' replied he, 'and I can gain no tidings of him.'

"'Thy servant,' replied the hostess, 'waits

not here; he was dismissed the instant he arrived'."

Trust a woman's wit in all such cases, thought I.

"Fearing lest the police might apprehend him for being out at such an unseasonable hour, my master took his departure in no very good humour, as I ascertained from the half-muttered curses that fell from his lips. The fair widow, nowise disconcerted, rejoined me."

I pass a veil over the sequel of this portion of Jim's narrative.

"On the following morning," continued Jim, "the exhilaration produced by the wine, the novelty of the situation in which I had been placed, and the luxuries which had been so profusely showered on me, had passed off; the usual reaction followed—I was in despair. Not so the widow. At early dawn she despatched a messenger to my master, inquiring the cause of his intrusion at her dwelling at such an unseasonable hour, threatening, at the same time, to report him to the Cazi of the quarter for his misconduct. His answer was in a deprecatory tone, promising that no further molestation should be offered. For myself, I was well pleased to exchange a good master for a better mistress. Here I remained for nearly a month, when the plague made its appearance. I should have before mentioned, that my mistress very shortly made me acquainted that, although outwardly professing the Mahomedan creed, she was at heart of the faith of her kindred. Hence arose the circumstance of our eating our meals together; and hence some portion of the attachment she was pleased to express towards me.

"Means to prevent the introduction of the plague were not neglected by my mistress; and I will give you an instance of the extraordinary strength of mind which she displayed in order to effect this purpose. Finding that no injunctions on her part could prevent the servants from stealing out, at the risk of bringing the infection within, she, with the exception of the Nubian servant, discharged the whole of the remainder of her household, bidding them, when the pestilence should cease, to return to their home. In vain they entreated, in vain they promised a most implicit obedience to her will; she was inexorable, and they were forthwith ejected. I was too young to feel any apprehension of danger, and Zuleika was equally devoid of fear. About midnight, seven days after she had discharged her servants, what was my horror to discover, on awaking, that she who had placed her affections so devotedly on myself was seized with fever; and the Nubian being summoned, he immediately informed me it was the plague.

"I knew not what to do: for seven days and as many nights I watched unceasingly at her side. At that time the disease appeared to take a favourable turn, and I had some hopes of her recovery; but these were speedily dispelled, and I had the mournful satisfaction, but a few hours afterwards, of performing the last sad offices to her remains. I was not so young but that I felt acutely the bereavement of the only creature who had treated me with affection. For two days I was in a state of stupor. Where and how was I to flee? The intelligence of her death speedily reached the magistrates, and the whole of her effects would of necessity be surrendered as a perquisite to the government. How I escaped the malady I know not; but I was in excellent health, and, as I have before mentioned, felt no apprehension. The very day my mistress had been smitten by the malady, she pointed out to me the place in which her treasures were lodged. Proceeding to that apartment, I secured a bag of gold sequins, and bidding the Nubian adieu, I speedily and silently quitted the house.

"With this I was enabled to procure a passage to Malta, and, after an absence of seven years, found my family in great distress, very inconsolable, as they told me, for my loss; but soon was such sorrow turned to joy when they beheld the gold. My earliest recollections induced me to believe that I was a favourite with all my family, save one; that one was a younger brother; he differed from me in complexion, and more in disposition. What reproduced his angry feelings I know not; whether it was that his ire was aroused at witnessing my better success in life, or whether it was that his cupidity was excited by the desire of possessing the gold, is equally uncertain; but very certain is it, that about midnight, two days after my arrival, I was awakened by finding a hand searching beneath my pillow, where, for greater security during my slumbers, the treasure was usually deposited. I opened my eyes on my brother: in his right hand he held a Maltese dagger.

"'Speak but one word,' said he, as soon as he perceived he had disturbed me, 'and that moment is your last.'

"Resistance would have been useless; so I was obliged to surrender the gold, and thought myself fortunate to escape with life. You will readily imagine that little sleep fell to my share that night. My brother had decamped at early dawn. I could not be a burden on my friends, so I strayed down to the beach, where I met a young friend I had known as a child, who was equally destitute and reckless as myself. There was at the time a small skiff riding at anchor, just without the curl of the surf, and it was, after some discussion, agreed between us that we should seize upon her, and proceed to the Syrian coast. No one was within the boat, and we effected our purpose without difficulty. About half way across, however, a schooner picked us up, kept our boat, and turned us adrift on this coast. Here we supported ourselves by fishing, until one day my companion venturing out too far from the beach when I was absent, was drowned. Two days afterwards I found his mangled remains wedged in between two small rocks. I removed the corpse to the sea-shore, and covered it with the rounded stones which lined the beach. I was thus left alone, my only property being my fishing-net, when I fell in with you."

Thus concluded Jim's narrative. Jim, let me repeat, was an invaluable servant. With that peculiar aptitude of acquiring languages which characterizes his countrymen, he had picked up a competent knowledge of almost every tongue spoken by those amidst whom he had mingled, and was every where, on this account alone, of the utmost service to me.

To those who have never visited these countries, the variety of adventure crowded into my servant's life may appear improbable; but let it be recollected, where there is no hereditary nobility, where no stigma is attached to lowliness of birth, where he who plies on the Bosphorus as a boatman to-day may be elevated to the dignity of Grand Vizier on the morrow, such vicissitudes are by no means uncommon.

A stranger passes a Turk of the old school smoking his pipe, and apparently absorbed in thought. How strange, how varied have been the scenes in which he has most probably mingled. No nation has the misfortune to have the character of its inhabitants more mistaken than the Turkish empire. A more polished gentleman than a Turk of rank could not be found amidst people who bear the credit of being more civilized than the "barbarous Osmanli." We have pursued a cruel policy with respect to these, our oldest and best of allies. The "untoward event" of Navarino will be for ever a blot in the historic pages of England. How vacillating, how absurd has since been the interference we have exercised between the Grand Seignor and the wily Pacha of Egypt. If we wish to retain India, we must eventually possess ourselves of the latter country.

To return to our voyage. A fair wind carried us within the bay of Antioch. This portion of the Syrian coast is what sailors term "iron bound," the cliffs rising perpendicularly from an almost unfathomable depth. The summits and sides are fringed with dwarf pines, but no villages are seen, the whole of them being, to avoid the bleak winds, erected on the land side. At length, however, we espied a small fishing hámlet, and from its inmates we purchased some bread and cheese; with this we continued our voyage until we entered the bold and picturesque bay of Antioch; the wind then veered, and we ran in for shelter between two rocks, where we remained in safety for three days. Near the spot where our bark lay at anchor there were some fishermen's huts; we took possession of one of these, and the bottom of an old jar which we found served us, after we had contrived to make a fire, to cook the shell-fish which were every where strewn along the beach.

We at length got tired of this fare, and started

again, plying our oars all day. Towards the evening we were so overcome with the heat, that we let the boat drift on to the southern side of the bay, and there we again cast anchor. When all was snug, as our provisions were expended, we landed, with the intention of begging some bread at a hut which appeared distant about a mile from the beach. I laid down near the margin of the sea to solace myself with a pipe, while Jim proceeded alone for this purpose. While watching the declining sun tinting with his golden beams the now tranquil expanse of water before me, a half-waking dream conveyed me to home and friends. Suddenly I was aroused from my lethargy by the discharge of a shot at no very great distance, and springing on my feet, perceived Jim pursued at full speed by three Kurds. There was not a moment to be lost, and our first idea was to make for the boat; but the reflection of a second convinced me that would be more dangerous than remaining where we were. My pistols had been sold at Tripoli to raise money for our voyage; our only weapon in the boat was a short gun, and that was not primed.

Whiz now came two balls close past my ear, followed on the instant by the sharp crack of another gun. The three Kurds who had pursued Jim had come up, and for the moment we were safe. Jim was stripped in a twinkling, but my dress being of a more complicated description, I was compelled, to avoid the kicks and blows accompanying every unsuccessful effort on the part of the savages, to assist in disrobing myself. How wistfully I looked at and longed for one of the broad short daggers which they held sheathless in their hands. We were now joined by several other Kurds, and a debate arose as to the propriety of putting us immediately to death. I saw Jim, who understood their language, turn deadly pale, and had almost given up our case as hopeless, when we were released from our danger by one of those merciful interpositions of Providence which have so often during my wanderings been extended to me.

The Kurds were mountaineers, and could not swim. Our boat was about twenty yards from the beach, and they had been making unsuccessful efforts to reach her; we affected to be alarmed at such efforts, and Jim kept calling out to them in their own language that they would be drowned. I suggested to him, as we could both swim like fishes, that he should propose for us to swim off and bring her in. The savages at first refused, but eventually were silly enough to comply with this request. Being perfectly naked, we were in good trim for such work; and no sooner did I feel myself released from their murderous grasp, than I darted into the water, closely followed by Jim. He sprang in on one side and I on the other; in an instant the grappel-rope was cut, our oars were out, and our light skiff glided swiftly from the shore. It was near dark, and we had gained some yards before the Kurds understood our manœuvre; they then fired a volley, but only one shot struck the boat. We pulled all night, and on the following morning entered the Orontes river.

## CHAPTER IV.

Enter the Orontes—proceed to Antioch—quit the River—Storm in the Gulf of Scanderoon—Phosphorescent appearance of Sea—Boat capsized—Author's perilous situation—arrive at Scanderoon—its pestilential Climate—Incident—again visit Antioch—Description of that City—rejoin Jim—monstrous Fish—open a Shop, and retail Shoes and Sandals—hasty Departure—Land Travelling.

THE sea was breaking fiercely over the bar—not with that pellucid, sparkling, and clear curling wave which fringes other portions of the shore, but, dark, turbid, and sullen, they rolled onwards lazily and heavily to the strand. Our skiff was, however, light, and hoisting our sprit, we safely passed the barrier. Within, the water was perfectly smooth; and making for the right bank, which was the steepest, we cast a line on shore. Jim and I then took it in turns to tow the boat against the stream. The few inhabitants we saw, judging from our wretched plight, did not think us worthy of more than a passing glance; our garments consisting only of a tattered waist-cloth. Towards evening, our further progress was interrupted by a line of fishing-stakes, which extended completely across the stream. Here I left Jim in charge of the boat, while I walked to Antioch, then distant about eight miles. Upon stating my condition to the English consul, Georgius Deb, he generously furnished me with enough money to replenish our wardrobe, and purchase another anchor for the boat.

I remained in this city two days, nearly the whole of which was passed in repose. At the end of that period I bid my hospitable host adieu, and rejoined Jim. I found him looking sleek and happy; for, upon my first arrival at the city, I had not forgotten to dispatch to him an abundance of provisions, together with some *rackee,* of which Jim was passionately fond; he would drink it like water, and I never could perceive that it produced any sensible effect upon him.

During the period I travelled in these countries, I in general carefully avoided ardent spirits. There was, however, an exception, which formed so curious an incident, that I cannot resist the temptation of mentioning it here. Three Turkish soldiers, with whom I became acquainted in a coffee-house, and whose company I was desirous of retaining, that I might listen to the feats of love and war with which these bearded Moslems entertained me, induced me to proceed with them to a place where *rackee* was sold. We were shown into a private apartment, where we smoked and drank until long after midnight. A quarrel then took place between two of these worthies; they drew their swords, and were making fiercely for each other, when, to prevent further mischief, I knocked one of them down, in return for which kind office I was knocked down by his opponent, and we all three fell kicking, struggling, and cursing together. This is all I remember of the scene; for the host, hearing the disturbance, had turned us out into the yard, where we slept in the open air during the whole night.

Thanks to the purity of the climate, the only penalty I paid for my intemperance was a tremendous head-ache. When I awakened my companions, I found them quite well, and, after they had swallowed a few glasses of the fiery spirit with which we had been indulging on the previous evening, we were ready for breakfast. I often saw the three veterans afterwards, and whenever I did so, even their Moslem gravity gave way before any allusion to our evening's adventure.

The quantity these men drink is really enormous. I recollect an instance of a man in Muscat harbour, who, to the great delight of the Middies of the ship, would drink two tumblers of raw brandy without evincing any symptoms of inebriation; this was, however, rather too dear an experiment to be often repeated. The very prohibition contained in the Khoran seems, with the more indifferent Moslems, to increase rather than allay the indulgence of this vice.

The next morning we hoisted our sail, and, aided by the current, soon reached the mouth of the river. It was high water, and we had little difficulty in passing the bar. Following the coast to the southward, we passed the night at Suedea, where there are some ruins, but neither of magnitude, antiquity, nor importance. Here we replenished our stock of provisions, and on the following morning, after labouring at the oars for several hours, we doubled the head-land which forms the northern horn of the bay. After effecting this, a fine fair wind carried us to Rás Kumseen. Rounding this point, the wind, rushing up the gulf of Scanderoon, blew with so much violence, and raised so heavy a sea, that I expected every succeeding wave would curl up and fill the boat. In order to prevent this, Jim sat on the gunwhale, with a coat spread over his back, and more than once this expedient saved us from being swamped. In vain, as I looked around, did I seek some lone nook which would shelter us from the fury of the storm. The sun set beneath heavy masses of clouds, and there was every reason to believe it would not lessen during the night. There is but little twilight in these latitudes, and a murky darkness succeeded.

The whole of this part of the coast is studded with sunken rocks. More than once we passed within a few yards of such dangers, and could perceive the sea foaming and hissing around them as in a boiling cauldron. I never remember to have seen the sea more highly phosphorescent than it was on this night; the whole appeared one vast lake of fire, broken into more sparkling refulgence by the crest of a wave, or crossed by rapid flashes which fled past with the rapidity of a cloud's shadow on a sunny day.

Refreshed by my stay at Antioch, I enjoyed the excitement of our present situation. Taking my position at the prow, while Jim steered, I piloted our little bark in safety for several hours, until, either weary with watching, or from some other cause, I was at fault; the boat rose on the crest of a long curling wave, and was borne along with frightful rapidity.

"Let go the grapnell!" called out my companion, in a voice rendered shrill by fear. It was over the bows 'ere he had spoken; we held on for an instant, and but an instant; for the next surge, as we were striving to roll up the sail, which fluttered and filled to the blast, drove the boat for a few seconds before it, broached her to, and a quick succeeding wave completed the work, by hurling us over like a cork. . . .

"Stick to the boat!" roared Jim.

Very easy that, thought I, could I see it; but this the darkness prevented, our only light being the foam of the sea, and I could nowhere discern her. Anticipating the result, I had, fortunately, before the second wave struck us, seized an oar, and of this I kept a firm grasp. Wave succeeded wave, and I drove onwards I knew not whither, till at length one tremendous surge struck and threw me over on my back, nearly driving away my senses. I had swallowed much water, felt painfully sick, and inclined to relinquish my hold, and sink to death. By a powerful effort I recovered the tone of my mind, and convulsively grasped at the oar; but my senses were fast leaving me. At the moment I am penning these lines, the only recollection which I preserve of the matter is of a pleasing rather than a painful nature, such as might arise from the effects of a dose of opium—a half dreamy and wholly unconscious state. I have a distinct remembrance of my feet touching the ground, and of being carried by a receding wave again to seaward; but here my memory wholly leaves me.

Jim had come to the shore safe enough with the skiff, and at this time was hallooing aloud for his companion. Suddenly he caught a glimpse of my body, floating, as he afterwards described it, to and fro in the surf; he rushed in and bore me out, just in time to prevent a heavy breaker from bursting over us. Placing me then on my face in the sand, he tickled my throat with a straw until I vomited a large quantity of water. The first of my senses which I regained was that of hearing; the roar of the sea fell upon my ears like the loudest thunder; again I vomited, and again I felt better, but giddy and weak. I raised myself on my arm, but sank exhausted on the strand, and slept.

The warmth of the sun's rays, about nine on the following morning, awakened me; and rousing Jim also, who had been slumbering by my side, we sought our boat, and found that every thing had come on shore safely in her. Seeing at sunset the danger we were likely to encounter, I had taken the precaution to lash the dollars we had with us to the seat of the boat. Collecting a few dried leaves and sticks, we lighted a fire by means of a flint and steel which we each carried at our girdles, and then heating some water in an earthen jar, we, with a little tea left in a bottle well corked in the boat's locker, and some shell-fish, made a most hearty meal. This concluded, we again launched our skiff.

Jim had fared better than myself on the preceding evening; it was therefore arranged that he should steer, while I laid down in the bottom of the boat and slept. The only ill effect of my bath was a cold shivering, which took me some days to shake myself clear of. Towards sunset, feeling much refreshed by my slumbers, I took a turn at the helm, and the next morning found us at Scanderoon.

Scarcely had we anchored, than my very amiable friend, Fouranetti, then consul, who had received intelligence of our difficulties, dispatched a servant with a letter, requesting me to proceed forthwith to his house, and make it my home so long as I remained. Jim remained with the boat to proceed to Latakea, where I purposed to join him by land. I have but little to say of Scanderoon, or Alexandretta, as it is sometimes termed. It is the only harbour of

Syria where vessels can ride in safety, and would therefore hold a high rank as a station, did it not so happen that its pestilential climate debars people from living there. Yet this is in a great measure owing to the neglect of cultivation, and clearing the streams, which teem with decayed vegetation; for at the time of the Crusades it does not appear to have proved so insalubrious, as the Christians constructed a castle here, the ruins of which still remain. It is nearly surrounded by hills, and the intermediate plain between that range and the sea is filled with marshy tracts, which exhale so impure an atmosphere that not more than a dozen houses are now inhabited. The sea appears to be rapidly receding on this part of the coast, the inhabitants state about two feet every year; certain it is, that the castle of Bouillon, in the walls of which rings for fastening the cables of ships are still perceived, is now a quarter of a mile from the beach.

The repose of a few days enabled us to journey on to Bielan, where Fouranetti had a house, picturesquely situated in the gorge of a mountain pass. The air was keen and bracing, and the society of my host's wife, an Aleppee, did wonders towards restoring me to health.

It has been said than an author's style should

be the picture of his mind. I know not if mine is so; but no effort has been spared to make it as elastic as my spirits usually were while mingling in these busy scenes. Yet I occasionally paid the penalty consequent to poor human nature, such excitements being followed by corresponding depressions.

Under the influence of these nervous fits, I one evening walked forth, and strayed upwards towards the summit of the mountain. It was a lovely eve—all nature seemed reposing in quietude; I seated myself on a mound, and watched the falling waters of a small cascade, which with mimic fury were hurrying over a fretted rock, grey and time-worn, into a clear pool beneath. The sky was of that deep blue which is rarely witnessed but within the tropics, and imparted its colouring to the stream. I sank into a slumber, and when I awoke found the air piercingly cold; a lovely moon had risen, and was high in the heavens. I rubbed my eyes, and thought of my host, whose fears would certainly be raised by my absence; bathing my face, therefore, in the stream, I endeavoured to retrace my steps. The foliage occasionally was so dense as wholly to obscure the moon's rays from the path, and more than once I found myself within a few inches of the precipice.

About two hours after midnight, jaded and fagged, I reached the dwelling of the consul. He and his wife, much to my annoyance, had not gone to bed, but having despatched servants in every direction to seek for me, they were anxiously awaiting the news, entertaining, and with justice, some fears that I had been carried off by the robber hordes which infest these mountains. A word served to explain matters, and in the course of a few minutes we had adjourned to another apartment, and were seated around a capital meal, which my fair hostess had prepared for me. A gentle reprimand from her was all the penalty I paid for my indiscretion; and what with talking, smoking, and drinking coffee, we did not separate before daylight.

I passed a week in this agreeable society, and then, with unfeigned regret bidding my host adieu, I journeyed again to Antioch, taking up my quarters at first with my old friend Georgius Debb.

I must say a few words respecting Antioch. It was formerly the capital of an extensive province, but has now, from the population of 150,000 which it boasted during the Crusades, dwindled to less than a tenth of that number. One cause of its decay has been the frequent visitations of earthquakes: since the birth of our Saviour, no less than seven times has this city been completely destroyed. The extensive fortifications which formerly surrounded the present site are rent and broken into huge masses, which are strewn over the plains as if scattered by the winds; towers, of vast thickness, have been carried uninjured, save an occasional fissure, some yards from their original position.

Antioch is situated about fifteen miles east of the Mediterranean, and forty south-west of Aleppo. The river Orontes passes its walls; and though the stream is small, it supplies the town with a variety of fish, and serves to irrigate the surrounding country. Here are reared a vast variety of fruits and vegetables; in addition to which, Antioch exports silks, carpets, blue, red, and yellow morocco leather, gums, opium, mastic, emery, almonds, wine, oil, figs, raisins, &c. &c. The inland trade is carried on principally by Jews and Armenians; the inhabitants having few merchant-vessels, both their exports and imports are conveyed in foreign bottoms. Antioch contained one of the seven churches; and the Christian community still exhibit, with great reverence, a tower bearing the name of St. Paul, it having been honoured with a visit from that apostle.

I now became very anxious to know what had become of Jim and the 'Nancy,' and I journeyed to Latakea for this purpose, where I found both. Jim had much to communicate. While I was reposing myself, he had been fishing along the coast; and when he wished to return, a captain who had been engaged and paid for conducting our bark to Scanderoon, only towed it half way, and there, in the night, he cut the tow-rope, and left Jim once more to the mercy of the waves. After two days' voyage, Jim made the coast to replenish his water, where he had the misfortune again to encounter a horde of robbers, who stripped him of every thing excepting a pair of trowsers; and in this plight he reached Latakea. The robbers had also helped themselves to the jib of the boat, and I was obliged to purchase a new one. Generous as had been Georgius Debb's conduct to me, I did not wish to trespass further on his kindness; and I was therefore compelled to part with a horse which he had previously presented to me.

Again furnished with money, we cruised along the coast until we arrived at Tripoli. Absence had whetted rather than allayed the desire which I felt once more to behold the beauteous Anna. With a throbbing pulse and beating heart I sought the dwelling of the fair Greek; but guess my dismay when I discovered that the whole family had journeyed to Jerusalem, on a pilgrimage to the Holy Sepulchre. Jim, however, was not in love, and, of course, more reasonable than myself.

"Most respected Khalil Aga," said he, "our funds are small. Love is very well when you have lofty apartments, marble fountains, champagne, and all that; but you are too poor to remain in love—let us again catch and sell fish."

"Agreed, Jim," said I. So we forthwith purchased lines, and commenced our old avocation. Our life was now one of comparative idleness: during the day we lounged about the coffee-houses, and when sunset approached we debarked, and pursued our avocation, but without our usual success. One evening I had placed on my hook a very tempting bait, and was lounging half asleep in the boat, when suddenly my arm received a jerk, which nearly dislocated it, and the line was flying rapidly through my fingers, when Jim rushed to my assistance, and hastily took a turn round the seat, with the reel on which our line was spread. Whiz, went the cord, as the skiff, propelled at the rate of about ten miles an hour, dashed furiously forward, raising before us a wave that threatened to overwhelm us.

"Watch the line," said Jim; "keep it in the stem, and no fear."

I did so. For nearly an hour we held our rapid course. Occasionally the leviathan would approach nearly to the boat; every inch we could then gain was carefully gathered in, until at length we had nearly drawn in the whole. Still keeping my eye on the line, I saw the fish, which I now perceived to be the basking shark (about thirty-five feet in length) turn slowly from the surface, cut two or three capers with his tail, and down, down he went, bringing the boat's bow on a level with the water, which commenced rushing in at a rate that in five seconds would have filled us. The line was was cut both by Jim and myself at nearly the same instant.

"Such fish are not for us," said Jim, very coolly, as he drew forth from the locker another hook and line.

After this event we barely gained a subsistence. One day we caught a fine rock cod, and, at Jim's suggestion, I sent it to the British consul, under an impression that, according to Eastern usage, he would have returned three times the value. Most anxiously did I await

Jim's return, who had gone with the fish; he came, with a blank face—"A meal in the kitchen," said he, "is all the consul's hospitality I have shared." We never troubled bim again.

Notwithstanding our ill success, we continued to follow our fishing; for I always carried with me a line of Lord Byron's, worth a ton of philosophy—

"When things are at the worst, they sometimes mend."

One day we were more than usually successful; in fact, we filled our boat, and by the sale realized no less a sum than ten dollars. This was comparative affluence; so we hired a small shop, putting the boat up for a while.

Jim forthwith purchased and set about disposing of a stock of shoes and sandals. He was full of amusing banter, and was never chary of this with the ladies; and many very pretty damsels made their outward show of purchasing shoes an excuse for an hour's amusement with him. There was one lass with whom Jim was deeply smitten; she returned to him every morning, making each time a purchase of a pair of sandals. I was in the habit of sitting behind, and watching the passing scenes in dignified silence.

"That lady, Jim," observed I, "must walk a long way, to wear out so many shoes."

He smiled, but made no reply. Next day, however, I received an intimation from a friend to quit the city with as little delay as possible, as the husband had laid a trap to catch Jim; and failing that, had sufficient influence with the governor to make good any charge he might think proper to bring forward. Disposing, therefore, as quickly as possible, of our stock in trade, and our old companion, the 'Nancy,' we with the proceeds purchased a horse and mule, and sallied forth to travel by land.

## CHAPTER V.

Proceed to Khalat el Hassan—Reflections—Imprisonment for Debt unknown in the East—Taken as a Spy—sentenced to Death—pardoned, and quit the Town—Return to Aleppo—Valley of the Orontes—Theological Discussion—Enter Aleppo—Frequency of Earthquakes—Character of Inhabitants—Education—Propriety of Demeanour—Their Children.

We first directed our steps to Khalat el Hassan, a fort of considerable magnitude, distant about a day and a half from the coast. It is situated on a hill, and was built about the time of the Crusades. Here there are moats, drawbridges, portcullis, castellated towers, corridors, dungeons, &c. without end. Methought, as I walked about amidst them, how Mrs. Ann Radcliffe would have delighted to havè followed my steps.

The church remained in a tolerable state of repair; but the Moslems have left few tombs of the champions of the cross undefaced, and in some cases their bones have been exhumed. Hence I strolled to the principal dungeon; it was quite dark, and the soldier who accompanied me bore in his hand a torch. There were now, Heaven be praised! no tenants; but the rings, the worn floor, the half-rusted chains, the inscriptions on the walls, told quite enough. I shuddered as I thought of the cruelties which man inflicts upon his fellow man, and hastily motioning the soldier to quit the den, I hurried to the open air with nervous anxiety. Of all the cruelties which disgrace our nature, that of dungeon confinement is perhaps the most terrible—the most so when solitary. 'Tis true that time reconciles us to most things; that when bereft of all which made life dear, the prisoner may exclaim, with *he* of Chillon—

> " * * * * * Even I
> Regained my freedom with a sigh."

Most punishments are mild and gentle compared to this; and I am surprised to hear philanthropists speak of substituting it for that of death. Death is a relief to the wretched. No one commits a crime but under the influence of a temporary insanity. The godlike attribute of reason was given to man, like all that God has bestowed on animated nature, for a wise purpose—that he might differ, through its exercise, from the beasts of the field. A crime is committed under the influence of the thousand-and-one feelings and passions which sway the human breast. To deter others (for to this is to be referred the cause of all punishment), the offender suffers what is considered an adequate loss in proportion to its magnitude, either in person or by detention. If a man is hanged, his expiation is considered to have been perfect: the world, in its varied excitements, find other themes of curiosity and converse, and, beyond a record in the Newgate Calendar, or, perhaps, if a state prisoner, a paragraph in continuation of Hume and Smollet's History of England, he is speedily forgotten. But the poor immolated living corpse (for he lives but in name—*exists* might be a more correct term) has the gnawing worm at his heart, and the only relief he can pray for is, that another fit of monomania may reconcile him to his lot.

Imprisonment for debt is unknown where the Mahomedan religion prevails. Every person's circumstances become in consequence more fully known, and a man is rarely trusted beyond his means of repayment. It has often occurred to me, that if one of that creed were conducted to our debtors' jails, and there permitted to view the varied scenes of misery on the one hand—the riot, debauchery, and crime, on the other—and were then told that the incarceration of the greater number was continued because they could not pay, he would depart with a far lower opinion of our wisdom than we should feel flattering.

It was, however, impossible to gaze on the pile before me, and not feel other reflections arise, to carry the imagination back to that period when gallant knights and fair company enlivened its walls. The gay pageant of a tournament, its feats of arms, their best reward a woman's smiles and thanks, were well adapted to the barbaric taste of the period. Strange, however, is it, that the remnant of uncivilized hordes should have introduced a state of society more polished than that of the best ages of Greece or Rome, and which has endured to the present period, modified certainly by the refinement of after ages, but still in its essential features the same.

I was recalled from the contemplation of this scene by a fierce encounter between two of the guards. Before they could be separated by their comrades, one was so severely wounded by a sabre cut on his head, that it was thought he could not survive many hours. Such, too, was my opinion: a more fearful gash I never witnessed; the brain could absolutely be perceived beneath. Not a groan, however, escaped him. His wound was dressed in a rude manner; on the following morning there were very slight symptoms of inflammation; and in the course of a few days the man was pronounced to be out of danger. His opponent suffered a week's confinement, and was then bastinadoed, and discharged.

Nothing astonishes an European more than to observe, where care is taken, how quickly wounds inflicted on this people heal: their simple diet and temperate habits are admirably adapted to bring about such a result. Charcoal applications, together with saffron, &c. are on these occasions in great request, to which they occasionally add a few herbs; but seldom adopt what we should in every case recommend —frequent ablutions, and great moderation in diet.

The aga in charge of the fort behaved to us while we remained with much hospitality, and both Jim and myself fared sumptuously; we at length bid the party adieu, and journeyed on to Homs. Our wallets were well packed, our steeds had been exchanged for two of a better description, and, upon the whole, our appearance was far more respectable than when we quitted Antioch, and our spirits were proportionately exhilarated.

The intermediate country was barren, stony, and wholly uninteresting. Modern geographers state that this town occupies the site of Emesa. A Roman fortress still overlooks it, but is in a most dilapidated state. To this I had strolled, and was busily engaged copying some inscriptions in the Punic character, which were scratched on the walls; but ere my task was half completed a dozen soldiers came towards me, and uttered two brief words, "Follow us." Strange as all this appeared, resistance was useless, so I obeyed.

In my way through the town I observed every person quitting their dwellings and following our party to the *serai* of the governor, whither I was now led. A line of followers occupied the path to the door, where I saw three persons seated; two were advanced in years, the third was much younger. All was silent; I made my obeisance according to the Turkish form, my right hand placed across my breast, and bowing lowly and reverently.

"Who art thou?" was the first question demanded. This was one of those numerous questions, as Sir Walter Scott remarks, more easily asked than answered, and for an instant I was greatly at fault, but, recovering myself, I replied—

"I am an Englishman."

"You lie," responded one of the worthies of the divan.

"You an Englishman!—you are a spy from Egypt," replied the one who was at his elbow.

Now for the first time I perceived the cause of my seizure, and the rising of the people. Mahomed Ali at this moment was engaged in advances on Syria, and they were apprehensive that I was in his employ; my positive disclaimer was listened to in utter disbelief.

"Produce," said I, "my servant; look at this firman from the Grand Seignor, authorizing me to travel in his dominions."

Jim was sent for, but the document they treated with the utmost scorn; it was passed round, and then thrown by the young man indignantly in my face. Witnesses now showered in, and their evidence was taken; one deposed that I had picked up stones, another that I had written down the whole country. I produced my note-book. Jim was found, and examined at some length, but his evidence did not avail us; and the members of the divan came to a close conference; the mob was highly excited, and had they been our judges, our fate would at once have been decided. As I cast my eyes around, and beheld how savagely they regarded us, and how anxiously they were awaiting the signal which was to cut off two fellow-creatures from the world, I could not for a few seconds but reflect deeply and bitterly on our situation. Never did I feel less inclination to quit the world than at this moment; but a glance at my servant roused me; he had been fixing his gaze for some time on me.

"I hope," said he, breaking the silence, "they will not, master, impale us."

"God's will be done!" exclaimed I, "and not ours; but we can, since we have in vain declared ourselves English, but try what proclaiming ourselves Mahomedans will do."

With this *shiboleth* at hand, I determined to wait to the last minute. The deliberation of the divan at an end, the governor, who was the younger of the party, turned suddenly round, and passed with rapidity one hand over the other; a murmur of applause, and then a deafening shout, indicated that this signal for our execution was but too well understood. I looked wildly on the assembled multitude who were eagerly awaiting their prey, and then on the judges.

"Spare," exclaimed I, "the life of this lad, whose only offence is following me."

"Let him," said the governor, "who eats the bread of dogs, also die a dog's death."

The executioners were now summoned, and a few moments were left for me to address my Maker. Few but fervid were the words which escaped my burning lips; I was then prepared, and perfectly resigned to my fate. But the love of life seldom deserts us under any circumstances, however desperate, and the effects of nervous excitement similar to mine at this period are, to sharpen, in an acute and painful degree, the senses of seeing and hearing. Stern as was the aspect of my judges, I yet perceived a glance of compassion from the eldest of the three, accompanied by a single Turkish word indicative of regret. In an instant I rushed forward, caught the old man by the hem of the garment, and clasped his knees.

"Father!" exclaimed I, "behold thy son!"

Overcome by this passionate appeal, he turned away his head, and exclaimed—

"Oh! Frank, for thee I can do nothing."

"But I will not, father, let go thy raiment; thou knowest I am innocent. Already half in the presence of thy Maker, go not to him with my blood on thy head."

Again he cast upon me a look in which I read hope.

"Release thy hold, my son," he exclaimed, "and I will see what my influence will avail."

The room in the mean time was cleared of

all but about a dozen guards, who smoked their pipes as unconcerned as if nothing unusual had occurred or was about to occur. In about five minutes the old Turk returned.

"I have succeeded," said he; "but hasten forthwith from the town."

Some words passed then between him and the guard, who were disappointed that they did not have my raiment. Certain customs alter not in the East, and who does not recollect that our Saviour's raiment was the subject of contention with the soldiers who attended his execution.

Followed by the whole population, we were now led forth, and, urged by the excitement of the moment, even the females took a part in the insults which were heaped on our devoted heads. In vain I addressed them, in vain I adjured the people to abstain; words were useless, and a dogged sullenness took possession of me. A broad-shouldered villain hurled a brick-bat at me; stooping to avoid it, I stumbled and fell; then arose a great shout. Horses were in readiness, thanks to our beneficent friend, and as we mounted and rode away, several shots whizzed past, but harmed us not.

Continuing our ride for many hours, we arrived at a small caravanseria. Exhausted by our former exertions I laid down and slept; Jim watched over me, and as I awoke, he too fell asleep.

At length I fainted. The poor people amidst whom I now found myself were hospitable beyond description; they brought me milk, rice, and various dishes, but I felt too much exhausted and tired to eat. Those who have travelled much will fully comprehend the feeling to which I allude; the body, like the mind, becomes so overcome by excitement continued without cessation, that a nervous feeling prevents our seeking nature's gentle restorer— peaceful sleep. Few of my readers but at some period of their life must have experienced the feelings to which I allude.

Five days' quiet restored me to my wonted health and spirits, and I then again journeyed by the valley of Orontes to Aleppo. Picturesque and wild, how strongly the ravine contrasts with the burning plains around! Doves, partridges, and other wild fowl started from every direction as we approached. My companions, (and the caravan with which I journeyed was a large one) would not have permitted me to have brought any of these to the ground; I was therefore compelled to loiter behind, and take a chance shot when I could find one; and thus I contrived to live until we arrived at Aleppo. Several rich merchants accompanied the caravan, who, accustomed to mix with the world and its varied inhabitants, affected to despise all difference of faith.

It had been rumoured through the caravan that I was a Christian and an Englishman, and the day after quitting my late quarters, an old man rode up alongside and entered into conversation with me. Much as I wished on all occasions to avoid theological discussions while mixing in oriental countries with strangers, yet there was something in the tone of voice of the person who now addressed me so placid, so mild, so engaging, that for once I forgot my usual custom. I had no blind bigot to deal with; his acquaintance with the Hebrew writings was as profound as was his knowledge of the Koran. We beguiled our way for several hours discussing the respective merits of the two creeds of Mahomed and our Saviour, and I was surprised to hear him at length admit that his own religion was only adapted to the East. "But," rejoined he, in a spirit of tolerance which would do honour to any creed, "all God's creatures are the same; and like the varied perfumes of a bunch of flowers will be the diversity of offerings poured forth from any region, in whatever form, to our great Maker."

On entering an Eastern city, the traveller will be guided by circumstances. If desirous of becoming at once known, he will forthwith ride to the consulate, proclaim his name, and live as best befits him; if, on the contrary, he is desirous of remaining *incognito*, he either buries himself with the other merchants in some obscure part of the city, or coops himself up in a cheap *khan*. For once I departed from my usual custom, and adopted the former course. A soldier we crossed in our path readily conducted us to the consul's house, where a meal was quickly prepared for me.

But I found my host was a Jew, and in the receipt of a very small salary. I therefore took apartments in a *khan;* and as I had been enabled to renew my funds, I went forth and made the acquaintance of several Levantine families. To me their houses were always open, their conversation gay and unrestrained. For two months I remained here. The weather became excessively cold, and certainly was not adapted for travelling; but my old passion returned, and I felt a desire again to renew my wanderings. Not so Jim, who, disgusted with our narrow escape at Homs, explained to me that he would rather return to Syria. Fortunately, it was in my power to reward my faithful 'squire; but our parting was bitter: he cared not for the dollars which I gave him, were they twenty, thirty, or a hundred; his whole soul seemed to be absorbed in our parting. Poor Jim wept most bitterly; and I was much affected. What his after fate was I know not, since I never saw or heard of him again.

After Jim's departure I felt very lonely, and for several days rather increased than removed this feeling by confining myself to my *khan*. I was aroused at length from my apathy by one of those awful events which, when nature displays any deviation from her ordinary course, tend to shew, more perhaps than any other, the utter insignificance of man. But a few months before my arrival, an earthquake had visited Aleppo: in less than five minutes ten thousand human beings were summarily hurried into eternity: every where did the city bear evidence of the calamity. To avoid, as far as lay in the power of its inhabitants, the consequenes of these visitations, they construct their houses with the most ponderous masses of stone, supplying also (which seems a singular contradiction) the usual roof of wood by arches and domes of the same material.

When the Mahomedan power was at its highest, Aleppo was celebrated for the number of its mosques, its colleges, and charitable institutions. The greater number of those have been overturned; others remain rent and torn in a most singular manner; but the very few which are entire, exhibit all the delicate tracery and elaborate finish of the Saracenic architecture. An ancient wall, possibly of Roman construction, surrounds the city; the large fissures in which have been closed with loose stones.

But the chief ornament of Aleppo, like that of Damascus, is its gardens, which are watered by a small stream; but the water being turbid and muddy, adds nothing to their beauty. Here is reared the pistachio-nut, in such great request with the *cuisine* of the East. The greater number of the wealthier inhabitants have kiosks here, where they reside during the summer months. Their time is then passed in paying visits, and drinking coffee with each other. Feasts, to both males and females, are given in the open air. I never witnessed at these parties the public introduction of any spirituous liquors, although there is little doubt but that large quantities are consumed in private.

The inhabitants of Aleppo are considered by their neighbours to be insincere; yet they are very polite and accomplished, as well as fond of pomp and display. In one respect they certainly excel many other Orientals: the bath is in constant use with them; and the linen worn by the upper classes is always clean. The use of cosmetics is by no means uncommon with their women, who may constantly be observed washing themselves and their children in the brooks. I was also amused at witnessing the care they bestow on the education of their children, most of whom at an early age can read and write. They commence with teaching them to form their letters on the sand; a wooden tablet with white or red chalk is next used, and I have observed them substitute the blade-bone of a camel for a similar purpose. Their children are admitted at an early age to the councils of their parents, and this begets a gravity and degree of intelligence at once pleasing and interesting. You meet a lad by the road-side, in these countries; you put some questions to him regarding the news, the crops, &c., and instead of the stupid country lout who, in other countries, drawls out a reply which the inquirer is fortunate if he can comprehend, you are at once answered, and much to the point. Contrary to Solomon's precept, their children are rarely if ever beaten; a word or two of reproof from either parent is generally found sufficient; and it forms a very marked feature in their character that very few of those not the very dregs of the people go wrong; and most of them become respectable members of society. There can be no doubt but that this is in a measure owing to their early marriages: for a man may intrigue after that event, but cannot without scandal openly act the part of a libertine.

## CHAPTER VI.

Effects of Earthquakes—Dread entertained by the Inhabitants—Greek Lady—her Daughters—Author joins their circle—fearful Convulsion—Apathy of the Moollahs—a Prediction—People return to the City—Visitation of a second Shock—Escape to a Cypress Tree—quit the Tree, and seek the Females—meet them in the Gardens—quit for Damascus—Col. Chesney, and Steam Navigation *viâ* Euphrates—arrive at Bagdat, and quit for India.

I HAD taken up my abode at a very large *khan*, which bore the name of Jaffa. In the great earthquake of 1822, this edifice did not escape; one part of the building had been removed from the other, leaving a space between, and not one of the walls retained their original perpendicular position. Yet such was the ponderous nature of the structure, such the ingenious dovetailing of the stones, or their connection by bands of iron, together with the adhesiveness of the mortar, that, unless where they had been actually rent in twain, the masonry clung tenaciously together.

The room I occupied was one of many which led from a corridor extending the whole length of the building; a small window, closed by wooden shutters, enabled the tenant to look out on the busy square which formed the centre of the building. As I was never idle on such occasions, if I did not join one of the various groups, several persons were sure to be seated in my apartment. Every one brings his own pipe and tobacco, and coffee forms the only expense to which the host is subjected.

The earthquakes used frequently to form a prolific theme of discourse. I affected to deride the fears which all expressed at the idea of an approach of these destructive phenomena. "You will not say this," (in answer to an observation of mine,) "when you shall have witnessed one," replied one of the party, a merchant. "Those who come here at first express the same opinion as yourself; but few, if they stay sufficiently long, carry the same opinion away with them."

I felt at this time the same desire to witness an earthquake as a man may do who, while he regrets the destruction produced by an enormous fire, feels nevertheless the sublimity of the scene it gives existence to, and hurries to it. Some unaccountable feeling of our nature impels us to view scenes of terror and desolation, to the recollection of which we cannot, however, recur afterwards but with feelings of sorrow and regret.

I soon began to feel the full force of the merchant's observation. At night I often looked at the roof, which was arched, and composed of large stones, and thought what a miserable fate it would be to awake, and find oneself entombed beneath it. I found myself often listening, with far more attention than I at first evinced, to the oft-repeated tales of former disasters; and I passed, therefore, less of my time in the *khan* than I did formerly.

My principal inducement to loiter so long as I did here was the society of a Christian family, which occupied the chamber adjoining mine. They consisted of a Greek lady and her two married daughters: a Geneva watchmaker was the husband of one; the other's lord was absent on a trading voyage to Malta. We passed our time in such society very agreeably, and October arrived.

One morning I had awakened about sunrise, and was leaning with my hand on the carpet preparatory to rising, when suddenly I felt the whole building shake violently, with a crashing noise, conveying to my half-scattered senses a momentary impression of terror which I shall never forget. There was, however, no time for reflection. I hastily rushed to the roof of the house, where I found a great number assembled—my Christian friends in *deshabille*, and silently beating their breasts. A moment had not elapsed when the heavy trampling of numerous feet announced that the population of the whole town were hastening towards the gates: an universal silence otherwise prevailed, broken only for an instant by a faint scream of some female or child which had fallen, and was almost as instantaneously trodden to death by the crowd, whose only object seemed to be to gain the open plain. The noise of so many thousand footsteps resembled the flow of the ocean tide; and clouds of dust, mingling with the cold and heavy morning mists, arose in every direction.

The first impulse of deadly terror being past, several hardy muezzins mounted to the summits of the minarets, and their deep cry of "Alla, Alla, akbar!" was now heard above the shoutings of the men and the shrieks of the women, who had again found their voices.

My Christian friends were for joining the hurrying crowd, but a moment's reflection convinced me this would be attended with far more danger than remaining where we were; and I prevailed on them, by representations that it might perhaps be several years ere another shock was experienced, to stay. In the mean time I went below, and brought their cloaks; and at their earnest entreaty, after having enveloped themselves in these, I returned, and brought with me a bottle of ardent spirits, which even such delicate and beautiful females drank in a few minutes, and then requested me to procure more; but to this, thinking for the present they had had in all conscience enough, I refused assent.

By this time the sun had risen, and the dusky morning mist partially cleared away, so that I was enabled to obtain a view of the damage sustained by the surrounding buildings. The dome of an immense mosque near our dwelling had disappeared, and several houses were levelled or had fallen in; but the most remarkable fact is, that several of the minarets had lost the cupola by which they were surmounted, while the columns themselves were left standing. It is also very singular, and proves in a forcible manner how completely the mind is filled, on the occurrence of such phenomena, with fear for individual safety, that neither myself nor any of the party had the slightest recollection of hearing these buildings fall, although the crash must have been tremendous, and we were all awake. The watchmaker had disappeared, and his wife was inconsolable. But in the midst of their greatest afflictions people must eat: he had left some fowls behind in a basket; I cut the throats of two of these, obtained some vegetables from the same quarter, and made a stew, of which we all partook on the terrace.

The ladies slept but little, consoling themselves with another bottle of *raki*. I thought it better to remain on the upper part of the house, because I knew if it sank, from its extreme solidity, it would do so in large masses, and we should stand a better chance above than below them.

Before it was dark I ventured to sally forth from the house. Some of the most rigid of the Moslems scorned to quit the city, and were seated as calmly alongside their wares as if nothing had occurred: but there were not very many of this number. The Jews and Christians had fled to a man; and they were joined by the governor, and all who could find the means to follow his example. Of eighty thousand souls, the usual population of Aleppo, but twenty thousand slept within its walls.

The call to evening prayers was heard as usual from the mosque; I had the curiosity to look within one, the largest in the city; there were about six men and three females, all very aged.

The police and soldiery had not fled, and their presence was of essential service in preserving the property of those who had done so, leaving it, but for this protection, completely exposed to the mercy of several bands of robbers. One of a party of these wretches was caught endeavouring to set fire to the town. The punishment in every case was summary—the offenders were strung up to the first door which was of sufficient height to serve as a gallows.

In a Turkish town they do not wait until houses are burnt and sacked before the civil authorities will then unwillingly interfere; a subordinate in these uncivilized countries would immediately lose his own head, if he neglected on the instant to act, when the public peace is broken and private property endangered. In their worst political brawls, seldom is it that this rule is violated.

On the following morning I went without the walls, and a curious scene presented itself to me: the whole of this vast plain was alive, and clustering with human beings. Some had constructed rude tents, by spreading their clothes across sticks; others had bivouacked beneath trees, or within hollows of the rocks; here there was a group half naked, huddling together; there another, with garments of the most varied hue and description: all was distress, confusion, and dismay. Some were weeping bitterly for those who had disappeared, others were smoking their pipes as coolly as if nothing unusual had occurred. But the most singular feature of all was, that the Moslems, alongside the Christians, were joining in groups, in one common supplication to the almighty Disposer of events. Danger, next to death, is the best leveller of distinctions: but a few hours before, for either party to have met in the same temple would have been the cause of deadly feud.

I could not learn that the mortality had been very considerable. The greater number of deaths arose from the rush and crowd to the gate; those who once stumbled never rose again; and many were crushed ere the doors could be opened, the pressure against them being too great (as they opened inwards) for this to be done. By the presence of mind exhibited by the soldiers at one of the gates these calamities were in a measure prevented; they felt the shock, and without a moment's hesitation, knowing from dread experience what would otherwise be the result, they threw open the portals at once, and thus gave an outlet to the stream ere it should collect in a powerful body.

In the midst of the general danger and distress, it was curious to observe the little care which even the graver Moslems took, to preserve their females from the gaze of the public. Those who perhaps for years before had not quitted the precincts of the harem, were now to be seen passing, without attempt at concealment, from their temporary dwellings. An old moollah, on the second day after the earthquake, had the hardihood to predict that the city would be exempt from another visitation for at least fifteen days. He was a man who in such matters enjoyed a great reputation; and on the faith of his prophecy numbers began to return, the bazaars again filled, people went to the mosque, and all soon subsided to its former channel.

The fifteen days elapsed, sure enough, without any other visit; but, on the following night, between twelve and one, a more severe shock than the former effectually roused me. I was soon on my legs, and as soon had dropped on to another house, and hence into the yard. Here for a time I felt bewildered, but quickly recovering myself, I looked around; a lofty cypress tree was before me, on the lower branches of which I mounted, and for a time I could not believe but that it was a dream. A second shock was felt, that too forcibly told the reality. Then arose screams which filled the air; people ran to and fro, they knew not why. Several buildings had fallen, crushing those within or near them: over a low wall, when the grey of morning dawned upon us, I saw a group endeavouring to raise, by means of a rough lever, a huge stone which had fallen and nearly crushed a fine young man, about thirty years of age; the upper part of his body had been left unharmed, but the lower, like that of Milo, was chained. With justice it has been asserted, that the agonizing feelings pourtrayed in the Laocoon, more than words, tell the extremity of human suffering; the expression is probably unequalled, whether we regard the feelings of the father or the sons; but methought, as I gazed on the group assembled before the sufferer, and beheld his wife, a young and beautiful female, bending over him, that all was excelled by the extremity of woe which I saw depicted in her countenance. At length the party were successful in raising the stone, they closed around; I neither saw nor wished to see more.

With daylight came the wish to ascertain the fate of my female companions, and, great as appeared the risk from fallen arches and columns, I determined to procced in search of them. Little, however, at the moment did I feel apprehensive, and accordingly I traced my way along the corridor leading to the terrace. But no ladies were awaiting me; they had fled to the gardens; and so I returned disconsolate to the tree, at the roots of which I slept during the night.

No food had reached my lips, and the following morning found me cold and hungry; I, therefore, left my retreat and strolled away from the town, in search without its walls of some one whom I knew. I wandered nearly the whole of the day without effecting my object, but at length, wearied, hungry, and athirst, I approached a group who were merry, and great and unexpected was the pleasure I received at perceiving myself in the midst of my old acquaintances the Greek family: their rejoicing was for the lost watchmaker, who had, without any regard to the welfare or safety of his spouse, taken an early departure. With them I passed the night: and, on the following morning, all apprehension as to the safety of returning being at an end, we, with the greater portion of the assembled multitude, returned to the city. I was now quite sickened of earthquakes, and most heartily sighed again for the desert.

My time, too, since Jim had departed, passed heavier than before, and I at length quitted Aleppo to return to Damascus. I will not detain the reader with my journey to that city, since little of interest occurred on the route. Here I found directions awaiting, from the resident, to repair to Bagdat, and report all the several objects of interest and science which had come under my observation since I had quitted that city. Those details, for reasons which I have elsewhere given, I have refrained from presenting to the reader. Colonel Chesney, with far better means and ability, has done so, and none, I feel convinced, can follow his track and not yield the palm which successful merit, high enterprize, and unconquered perseverance, must claim for him and his gallant companions.

That the route by the Euphrates should be abandoned more hastily than its projected feasibility should have been resolved and acted on, all must regret: the more so, that recent and forthcoming events in the political world add hourly to the interest we feel in the countries through which it flows. Those at home are, however, so occupied with party discussions, that it is seldom sufficient attention can be drawn towards the most valuable of our dependencies—the Indian empire; hence the difficulty which arises with regard to the establishment of a general steam navigation between the Eastern and Western world. Volumes have been written to prove the utility and practicability of that which, from the first, was self-evident; for, great and manifold as are the improvements which the knowledge of this vast power has given to mankind, it will not prove the least, that the legislation, for the welfare of one hundred millions of inhabitants, will create a higher interest with the mother country than has heretofore been exhibited.

During the recent crisis in Indian affairs, when Russian intrigue set every engine at work to excite and influence those bordering the British dominions who were disaffected, and were seeking a pretext and opportunity simultaneously to rise against us; when Birmah, Nepaul, Caubul, and Persia, were clustering their hordes to await but one unsuccessful effort on our side to close around us; think of what incalculable advantage it might have been, had we but possessed a steam flotilla on the spot! What millions would have been saved during the late Burmese war, if such a navy had been at our command! Both that empire and Hindostan are intersected by numerous deep rivers, and the facility these would afford, independent of two thousand miles of sea-coast, of throwing a body of men suddenly into any given spot, would, we should imagine, even on the score of economy, by rendering this military force less burdensome, have induced its immediate adoption. But no; we have been, since the measure was first proposed to be carried into effect, it would appear, either experimentalizing or looking at the matter with indifference; for there is still no approach towards a regular communication. A spirited body of merchants have, despite the sage prognostications of its failures from those whose opinions were considered valuable, set on foot, and now are prosecuting, within a far more recent period, a continuous and profitable journey across the Atlantic, for the conveyance of mails and passengers. Yet little has been done for the Indian communication: the vessels hitherto sent are small, and unfit for the duty which requires them to face the south-west monsoon. Vessels of large power, certainly not less than a thousand tons, are the only craft which can be expected to prevail against such boisterous weather; unless, indeed, at the cost of a few days more space of time, vessels proceed to the southward, where the winds are moderate—a mode very strongly advocated by all those most capable of judging.

It is impossible for the thinking mind not to regret, in a subject of this kind, that the inhabitants of the three presidencies divide themselves into parties, as to whether the steamers should start from Bombay or Calcutta—whether Socotra or Aden should be a depôt, or whether that called the "comprehensive" scheme should not be so comprehensive as to exclude Bombay from the participation of any benefit in the scheme. All these minor subjects should be left to experience and after-discussion; first establish your line of steamers. It appears about as absurd for the people in Bengal to object to the steamers starting from Bombay, as it would be for Ireland or Scotland to object to a Mediterranean steamer quitting Falmouth instead of the ports of London or Edinburgh. Let us now, however, hope that no longer will the wishes of those of either hemisphere be delayed, in the bringing about a communication, at once general and effective, between the mother country and the fairest jewel of her crown.

When the Resident had inspected the several maps and the details of my different journeys, it was thought most advisable that I should proceed to Bombay, and lay them before the Governor in Council of that presidency. To that port I accordingly proceeded, and arrived there in safety in June 1830, after an absence of nearly four years.

# A VOYAGE

TO THE

# COAST OF ARABIA;

AND

# TOUR ON THE ISLAND OF SOCOTRA.

# CHAPTER I.

Maritime Geography—Captain Owen—Sir Charles Malcolm—his Encouragement of Geographical Pursuits—East-India Company—Discovery of Ancient Inscriptions—Author arrives at Cape Isolette—Effects of Terrestrial Refraction—Phosphorescent Appearance of the Sea—Fluctuation in the Temperature—Currents within the Gulf of Aden—Arrival at Morebat—its Prosperity—Seyd Mahomed Akyl—Ferocity of Bedowins—Arrival at Kisseen—Visit to its Chief.

THE present age may be said to be marked by rapid and manifold improvements in almost every branch of human knowledge; but in none have these been followed up with more eminent perseverance and success than those tending to the advancement of geographical science. In that department, more especially, which has been styled Maritime Geography, so rich a harvest has been reaped, that we may now assume the principal points of the earth's surface to be correctly fixed; and of the vast unknown field which the seventeenth century exposed to the research and adventurous spirit of the navigator, little more is left for the gleanings of modern research, than the filling up of the intermediate detail. The indefatigable exertions of Captain Owen, which no deadliness of clime, no privation or labour, could effectually check, have at length added the greater portion of Eastern Africa to our maps; and the most important of other remaining blanks, whether we regard its extent or the interest attached to the name it bears, was that which forms the southern coast of Arabia, extending from the entrance of the Persian Gulf to that of the Red Sea.

England, it is usually supposed, regards her Eastern possessions with apathy and indifference; and Mr. T. B. Macaulay's celebrated taunt, "that a disturbance amidst the Spitalfields weavers excited more attention in the Senate than the legislating for one hundred millions of its native subjects," had some foundation in truth. But it is very certain that the same apathy and indifference does not extend to the interesting countries by which India is surrounded; the very name of Arabia, the country of Abraham, Isaac, and Jacob, calls up an echo from every bosom.

It may here be necessary to apprize our readers, that the East-India Company, for some years past, in addition to a trigonometrical admeasurement of the vast continent of India, have been silently and unostentatiously carrying on a series of nautical surveys, more extensive than were perhaps ever undertaken by any power before; that, under their auspices, has been completed a correct delineation of the sea-coast of the vast continent of Asia, extending from the Straits of Bab-el-Mandeb to the limits of the Yellow Sea—nearly fourteen thousand miles.

It is to be regretted that the principle which induced such munificent and princely undertakings should not have been carried a little farther, and have held out encouragement, or enjoined those entrusted with these duties, to give descriptive memoirs of the shores on which such operations were carried on, instead of leaving us, as we are in many instances at present, with nothing but the maps before the world.

That eminent and excellent hydrographer, Captain Horsburgh, sometimes in a foot-note acknowledges the labours of the officers of the Indian navy, as a source whence he obtained much of his information; and, more recently, some papers furnished by myself and brother officers in the "Journal of the Royal Geographical Society," on the geography of the Red Sea and Persian Gulf, have drawn the public attention to the omission in other quarters.

As there are neither astronomer, naturalist, nor, beyond the surveyors, other scientific men attached to these vessels, it is more than can be expected from the captain, however able or willing he may be, in every case to furnish such memoirs—embracing, as they should do to give them a proper value, much of the physical geography of these regions. His time is better occupied in watching over the navigation of the vessel, constructing the charts, or other duties of a maritime survey. Charts, however, continued to pour into the hydrographer's office, accompanied or not with descriptive details, but few or none of the latter were given to the world.

This was the state of affairs when Admiral Sir Charles Malcolm arrived in Bombay, to fill the office of Superintendent; and, in order to remedy the evil as far as lay in his power, not only were the commanders of surveying vessels directed to collect information on all subjects within their reach, but they were also expressly directed to afford facility and encouragement to officers desirous of proceeding to towns, and other objects of interest on or contiguous to the sea-shore. Their reports were received with the attention they merited, and the establishment of a Branch Society of the Royal Geographical Society offered every facility for the transmission of those of paramount interest to the mother country. Within these last few years nearly a third of the information printed by this Society, of their proceedings, has been furnished by the officers of the Indian navy.

In noticing the omission I have before alluded to, and which is too important to be passed over in silence, we must not forget the eminent claims the East-India Company have in other respects on the gratitude of their country. These operations have been steadily carried on in periods of financial pressure, which have called for powerful reductions in other quarters. In Europe, such expeditions shed an equal lustre on those who originated as on those intrusted with the execution of them. Perhaps George III.'s reign will be best remembered by the encouragement it afforded to geographical pursuits and discoveries. If, therefore, the state receives its full meed of praise for such undertakings, we surely ought not to withhold it from a body of subjects acting on principles equally noble and princely.

On these points Major Rennel, in his "Geographical Memoirs of Hindoostan," judiciously remarks—"That the employing of geographers and surveying pilots in India, and the providing of astronomical instruments, and the holding out of encouragement to such as should use them, indicate at least a spirit somewhat above the mere consideration of gain. But, above all, the establishment of an office at home for the improvement of hydrography and navigation, and their judicious choice of a superintendent for it, reflects the highest honour on their administration."*

To look back, therefore, on the past exertions of this colonial service of the East-India Company, to consider the heat and enervating nature of the climate, and the jealous and hostile character of the several tribes who possess the greater part of the country, it is very evident that more than ordinary energy and skill must have been exercised to surmount them. Varied, however, in language, character, and disposition, as are the tribes and nations in this extensive portion of the earth—a sixth of its whole outline—there is not an instance, I believe, on record, where a life on either side has been sacrificed by violence.

If we again turn to Africa, and see at what cost our knowledge of its coast was obtained, and that from Mogador to Cape Gardefui, its chart may be literally said to be drawn with

* Preface to the 2d Edition, p. 5, published in 1792.

the life-blood of those engaged in its construction; that Captain Owen, in its progress, lost nearly two ships' companies; and that Captain Vidal at present is hardly more fortunate; it is scarcely possible to view our dear-bought knowledge but with a sigh.

If, therefore, owing to a variety of causes, the information transmitted to us by the officers of the Indian navy has been obtained on coasts of equally bad repute, without a sacrifice of more, if in some cases as much, of the ordinary mortality, doubly, as men of science and as benefactors of the human race, are our thanks due to them. It is very true that the better portion of their lives are passed in these climes, and that experience has taught them what to practise and what to avoid; but they are not, as a body, the less entitled to our gratitude on that account. By judicious ventilation, by allowing the men cricket, and other athletic games on shore, at every possible opportunity, we remained within the Red Sea for twenty-two months, and did not during that long sojourn lose, of nearly one hundred souls, a single man.

In 1833, the Palinurus had just returned from an arduous and perilous survey of the Red Sea, many of the officers of which had previously been engaged on a similar examination of the Persian Gulf. To complete our knowledge of the whole ocean frontier of Arabia, the intermediate coast between the two seas alone remained; and with this view, and as much to seek for some well-sheltered harbour that would answer for steamers in their progress to and from India, she was again despatched from Bombay. I was appointed to her as assistant surveyor.

Some seventy years ago, the accurate and intelligent traveller, Niebhur, informs us, that the towns in Hydramaut and Yemen were better known to the ancients than the moderns; and so it continued until our expedition was appointed. The whole of these two provinces, though deficient in many of the storied recollections which invest the shores of the Red Sea, have nevertheless eminent claims on our attention. In the province of Hydramaut, the Homerite dynasty flourished for two thousand years, their dominions extending to India, and numbering amongst their monarchs the celebrated Queen of Sheba. Here also the first branch of that extensive commerce between the Eastern and Western world originated; while at a later period, deterred by the intricate and dangerous passage up the Red Sea, vessels contented themselves with landing their cargoes in its several ports, from whence they were, by overland routes, conveyed to Egypt and Syria. One of these routes, leading to the ruins of Nukub-ul-Hedjer, together with an extensive fort or magazine, I was fortunate enough to discover and trace for some distance—a discovery the more important, that Heeren and other antiquaries who have illustrated caravan tracks in Asia, have sought amidst existing authorities in vain for these. My journey on this occasion was also rewarded by the discovery of certain inscriptions in a character the decipherment of which is at present engaging the attention of Gesenius, and bids fair (in throwing open to us the history of these little-known regions) to be attended with the happiest results.

At an earlier period, Arabia the Happy seems to have merited the appellation she enjoyed; but when the current of the Indian trade, influenced by the discovery of the Cape of Good Hope, changed its direction, her commerce naturally declined. Yemen in a measure recovered itself by the exportation of coffee, then a new discovery; but Hydramaut, in its scanty exports of gum, &c., had no means of doing so. Navigators have, moreover, kept aloof from a coast which in the south-west monsoons, from

Aden to Ras-el-had, is a dead lee-shore. The currents, too, were rapid, and their set unknown. A further motive for avoiding it was the character of the inhabitants, who have with justice borne the reputation of being ferocious and hostile. At Morebat for many years resided a pirate chieftain, Seyd Mahomed Akyl, who plundered an American vessel and murdered the crew. In 1715, the Nathamal is described to have had a boat's crew cut off; and even as late as 1827, a vessel was seized in a similar manner and carried into Macullah; but the resident of Mocha very quickly compelled that people to restore her. From these several causes the geographical positions of this coast, from the entrance of the Persian Gulf to Aden, a distance of 1,200 miles, were inferred from various and inaccurate sources,* and in some places the error of position amounted to more than a degree.

After touching at Muscat, a tedious voyage conducted us to Cape Isolette, where we anchored, to await the arrival of our tender. The Cape offers but little shelter, and the vessel rolled and pitched the whole time with much

* Principally Lieut. Lewis, of the store-ship Prudence, attached to Admiral Blankel's expedition; Captain Moresby, in H.M.S. Menai; and Mr. Lumley, in H.M.S. Topaz.

violence. The coast is bold of approach, and a heavy surf lashed against it. Moderately elevated, it presents a succession of bluffs with horizontal ledges, the lower portions projecting so as to resemble enormous buttresses. Low sandy beaches connect these, and from a distance resemble bays, but our launch despatched to survey found no anchorage.

So near to the continent of India, it seems strange the natives of this part of Arabia know so little of our power. Two of our boats despatched very early to survey, on rounding a point, came unexpectedly at dawn of day on a large native vessel filled with men. Observing a general movement on board, the officer in charge had the small arms concealed, but in readiness. The Arabs most wantonly, in passing, opened a fire on the party; the shot fell in every direction, but no one was wounded. To return the volley and give chase was a work of but brief space. Compelled to pass between the ship and the land, two or three shots brought their boat to anchor just without the surf, through which they swam to the shore. The natives, attracted by the firing, had collected and opposed their landing; and our launch, with a three-pounder, was about to destroy their boat, when they compelled a slave to swim off with a passport from the Imaum of Muscat, and an apology, stating that they mistook the boats as belonging to some shipwrecked vessel. The rogues were very happy to get clear, and will not perhaps be quite so ready on another occasion.

Already in desert tracts I have had occasion to remark on the effects of terrestrial refraction. On the sea-coast they are not the less curious and interesting.

In the morning, as the disk of the sun emerged from the horizon, it would often assume a variety of forms: now a flattened oval; now, as it rose higher, either semi-diameter of a pyramidal outline; and again, as it still ascended, that of a flattened column. It was frequently eight or nine degrees high before the outline was perfect. A bank about two degrees in altitude is the limit of other distortions, and within that every object seen through the haze looks as if drawn on blotting-paper—all is indistinct, and acquires a tremulous motion; the outline is constantly changing, and occasionally, about every five minutes, a stronger or fainter glow is emitted, the light and dark portions then shewing out with peculiar brilliancy. I have known those banks occasionally rear themselves between the ship and the shore, and represent portions of the land so distinctly, that had we not sailed over the spot we could have sworn to the existence of islands there. Thus it is that navigators have been deceived, and that, especially in former years, our charts have been studded with reefs and islets near to the coast, which after examination, it has proved have no existence.

We passed an idle time here, the surf not permitting us to land, and the commander was also perhaps apprehensive of the Bedowins, who are of the Geneba tribe, bordering on the Beni-bon-Ali, to the eastward, and the Mahara to the westward. Occasionally they would come off to our boats, on two inflated skins with a board placed across, on which they seat themselves and catch fish. A stone serves them as an anchor. Sometimes they hook a large shark, and if they do not speedily despatch it, they are obliged to cut it loose, for the fish invariably makes for the ocean. None of them would venture on board.

Much has been written about the phosphorescent appearance of the sea, and yet we seem to have arrived at no very certain conclusion. There are secrets on the surface as well as within the bosom of the ocean, which lie shrouded from human observation and research. The fancy of our poets has peopled its coral caves, and my Arabian neighbours will beguile the midnight hour with tales of Peris and less agreeable personages, who in their belief also inhabit it. Where there is mystery there will always be interest, and the greater the one, the more intense the other.

One evening I was beguiling the tedium of the first watch, in conversation with an Arabian pilot; we were both leaning over the gunwale, and watching the extraordinary appearance of the phenomena I have alluded to. It was a gloomy night. Within these parallels in general we can discover the horizon sufficiently distinct to determine the latitude by the stars, but the limit of neither sea nor sky was now discernible; all was a murky void. Suddenly the extreme verge of the horizon would become tinged with light, which spread its effulgence as it flew towards us; the instant it came in contact with the vessel's side, it, as if arrested by the shock, again fell back, and all was gloom as before. When a portion passed the vessel, it as quickly disappeared; again it would approach in broad illumined bands, passing us with the same startling rapidity. It was calm, and what in these instances caused this velocity of motion? There was no current.

We may look in vain perhaps for these causes, as we may for those of another remarkable phenomenon, which is often alluded to by our earlier navigators, yet never, as far as I know, have they attempted to offer an explanation. At sea, perhaps hundreds of miles from land, the look-out will announce broken water in a certain direction, which, although it may be a calm, approaches with the same rapidity; small fragments of wood or rubbish are hurried along with it as it passes the vessel, and then all is calm as before.

"Seyd," observed I to the pilot, as one of these phosphorescent flashes passed us, "what is thy belief?"

"Alla aruph" (God knows), said he.

"That I am fully aware of," I made answer; "but what do your countrymen say to such appearances?"

"They never think of them—why should they do so?"

"Well, God is great," said his companion, who was staying on board with him. "I have heard an old man of my own tribe speak of such things. He was cast away in a pilgrim ship voyaging from India to Mecca, in the lower part of the Red Sea. As she was going down, he clasped a bag of flour, to which he clung for two days. It fell calm, and during the night, being almost senseless, a flash of these lights aroused him. He looked, and lo! he was drifting slowly by a rugged islet, a projecting point of which he was fortunate enough to cling to, and in a few moments to ascend."

It was evident that my friend firmly believed that such lights were created to succour shipwrecked mariners. I was once saved from a similar disaster in the Red Sea, by a heavy breaker, which, from its intense brilliancy, pointed out to us at night a hidden rock, over which it was bursting, and of the existence of which we were before wholly ignorant.

Our tender, for which we had been waiting for some weeks, at length arrived, and we weighed with a strong land wind for Morebat. Gradually it increased, until we were reduced to close reefs. These breezes are much dreaded by the Arabs, as they come on quite unexpectedly, and frequently drive their crazy barks to sea, where a miserable death by hunger and thirst await them. They usually set in about sunrise, increasing in strength until mid-day, and again dying away as the evening approaches. At first, from sweeping over the desert, (where the over-heated sultriness of the day is exchanged for a piercing coldness) they are bleak and unpleasant, but they warm as the day advances. Water retained in iron tanks within the hold exhibited this fluctuation in the strongest manner; throughout the day it indicated eighty-two degrees, while the temperature of the atmosphere fluctuated from sixty-five to ninety-five degrees Fahrenheit.

There are few portions of the globe where the results of calms and strong currents are felt conjointly with more effect, or in a greater degree, than within the Gulf of Aden. Here vessels have not unfrequently been drifted about, wholly at the mercy of the latter—now carried to the Abyssinian, and again hurried back to the Arabian coast, until they have been subjected to the greatest privations. One of the Hon. Company's vessels was thus entrapped for eight weeks, and was eventually compelled to destroy her casks, her spars, her boats, and lastly her gunwale, for fuel, with which they distilled fresh water from that of the sea. These currents would appear to obey no certain laws; sweeping up the coast of Africa to the northward, at a velocity of sometimes eighty miles a day, they impel a body of water into the Gulf of Aden, increasing the level of its waters, until a north-westerly breeze forces them to the southward, at a rate of almost equal velocity. Yet, after passing the island of Socotra, but little comparative drift is experienced, as we proceed to the eastward the whole becoming absorbed in the vast waters of the Indian ocean.

It has often appeared to me singular enough that tradition should have informed us that Hippalus first ventured across in the south-west monsoon, from the Red Sea to the shores of India, and hence that atmospheric current obtained the name of the Hippalean wind; he is, moreover, described to have sailed direct across, and in the worst month of the year. I have on several occasions passed the island of Socotra, lying in his route, on my way to India, at these periods, and such was the strength of the gale, the high and dangerous nature of the sea, that even we, in a stout vessel, apprehended considerable danger. How he, in his rude misshapen bark, could have safely accomplished the passage, must ever remain a mystery. I cannot but think that they are mistaken in dates, and that the earlier or later periods of these periodical winds must have been selected, when their force is not so great.

The size of a vessel does not, however, in a heavy sea, appear to be of much moment. One of Vasca de Gama's ships, which successfully encountered the heavy Cape gales, was but twenty-five tons; and that size, if the vessel is properly ballasted, masted, and manœuvred, is as safe as one of five hundred. In our survey of the Red Sea, we frequently encountered the heaviest gales of that region, and its heavy breakers and highly dangerous seas, in open boats, twenty-seven feet long and but seven feet in breadth, and not an accident occurred during the whole period.

We arrived at Morebat on the 19th December. It has been one of the most extensive and best sheltered harbours on the coast. The ruins of an old castle, a few wretched houses and still more miserable huts, shew themselves on the margin of the bay. Within, at anchor, were a few boats, which trade to India in gums, aloes, &c. These are produced on the high mountain range, which rises at the back of the town, and which, by means of our glasses, we could perceive was very thickly wooded.

When we anchored, a party of natives came on board; they were wild and uncouth beings, their features possessing a peculiarity which would render them very easily distinguished from the Arabs of other parts of the Peninsula. They were very dark, the nose thin, long, and projecting; the chin very broad, the eyes deep-seated, and the hair, though worn long, not plaited.

Morebat at one time enjoyed a considerable trade, and hence acquired the conspicuous place it has on our maps; at present the number of inhabitants does not exceed five hundred, and they are completely under the control of the Bedowins. The few traders who reside here were loud in their complaints against this class, declaring that no man's life was safe amidst them. An Indian who had belonged to the ships of Turkey bel Mass at Mocha, and had escaped to this place, was received on board the 'Palinurus;' he shewed a wound on his arm, which he had received in defending his turban; and a native of Hydramaut told me he was in hourly expectation of losing his life for the sake of the few tattered clothes on his person.

Seyd Mahomed Akyl, whose exploit in seizing an American vessel and murdering her crew I have already noticed, resided here for some years; he first took his prize into Camaran, but, apprehensive there of British interference, he removed to Morebat, the existence of which appears then to have been almost forgotten. Here he devoted himself to other pursuits, and endeavoured to make himself master of the whole country. For this purpose he intrigued with several of the tribes, and collected together a body guard of three hundred African slaves; he built a fort, mounted a few guns, and contrived for some years to overawe the whole country; but the Bedowins contrived at last to slay him, and to disperse his guard. It was a brother of this chief who preached at Mecca a crusade against the occupation of Egypt by the French, and who afterwards led his countrymen to that country. They met the invaders near Thebes, and Denon gives a vivid description of their charge, and inveterate courage. Nearly the whole party was cut to pieces.

Very good water may be obtained at Morebat, a few sheep or goats, and the common vegetables of the country; but ships putting in there for these necessaries, should keep a strict look-out on their Bedowin visitors. From the inhabitants of the town there is nothing to fear; but the former would glory in such an exploit as plundering a vessel, and then would away off to their mountains, perfectly safe from retaliation. A Bedowin here is rarely met with alone, but they walk about in groups of ten or twelve. In the evening, when their prayers were to be repeated, they would plant themselves in a line, unsheath their swords, and place the naked blades upright in the sand; before these, in the direction of Mecca, they prostrated themselves whenever the form of their prayers required them to do so.

A party from the ship, under the guidance of

these men, journeyed a short distance from the beach, and passed the night within one of their huts; they were treated with much hospitality. They described the country as being crossed in every direction by torrents from the mountains.

We remained in this harbour until our water was filled up, and were again ready for sea. The day before leaving, a relation of the sheikh died, upon which four bullocks, previously kept in readiness, were slaughtered, and distributed to all who came for a portion. The same custom prevails in Socotra. There, on one occasion, an old Arab had made similar preparation to do honour to his wife, who was very ill, and expected hourly to die; but before this event could take place, the husband himself became defunct, and the wife survived to transfer her intended honour to him.

We left the harbour December 29th, and the following morning found us off Dafar, a small town and fort which give their name to the contiguous district. A boat despatched for supplies reported favourably as to the facility with which they might be obtained; that water was plentiful, and cultivation carried on to a considerable extent. I think a more minute examination will determine that there are several small rivers on this part of the coast; for some openings said to be such were pointed out to us; and one, about eight miles to the westward of Dafar, appeared to discharge a large quantity of water into the sea. The natives here speak a very corrupt and barbarous dialect, and it is painful to see them converse, so hideous are the contortions necessary to give the gutturals their full power.*

We next passed Ras Furtak, a majestic promontory, forming the south-west extremity of a deep bay. Villages occasionally shew themselves on the margin of the sea, with the usual accompaniment of a line of date trees, and perhaps a solitary fishing vessel at anchor before them. There was too much swell for the vessel to enter the bay of Kisseen, and she was therefore anchored under a small cape about seven miles to the westward of Kisseen town. Abreast our station there was a small fishing hamlet, situated in a hollow; the huts were of a conical form, and covered over with mats, the Arabs in this and on other parts of the coast only requiring them during the fair season; when the rains set in they take refuge in the caves amidst their hills, subsisting on fish they have cured for the purpose.

* Some lengthened discussion on this dialect has already been presented to the reader in a former part of this volume.

It was proposed that some negociations should be opened with the chief of Kisseen, for the purpose of procuring assistance in examining the island of Socotra, to the sovereignty of which he lays claim. The projected establishment of steam navigation had drawn attention to this island, which it was supposed would from its position prove valuable as a coal depôt. Camels were prepared for me on shore, and I left the ship on this mission. Before we quitted the hamlet a quantity of small fresh fish were placed on mats before our camels, and were instantly devoured by them. Such, indeed, I am told, forms a staple article of their food at all seasons. An oil is expressed from these fish, (which resemble the Mediterranean sardine,) and is used for a variety of purposes.

Midway between the hamlet and the town there is another small village, with several fields of *jawari* in its vicinity, which were irrigated from wells, the water being drawn up by camels. Rarely is it that this animal is used for purposes of draught, the formation of its body and limbs being quite opposed to such a purpose. An old pilgrim, who had journeyed from Kurdistan to Mecca, joined the party here, and solicited our charity: the whole of this distance he had performed on foot. Two years had already been consumed since he set out; and he reckoned a third or fourth might elapse before he again entered his native city. A stout lad accompanied him; they subsisted wholly during these perilous journeys on charity, their poverty, indeed, being their only protection.

About a hundred houses, half buried in sand, are all which remain of Kisseen. Perhaps half a century had elapsed since any European had made his appearance there. I made my way to the Sheikh's residence, a large building, into which we gained admittance by knocking with an iron ring at the door. It was opened, and I nearly broke my legs over an iron gun placed in the middle of the staircase, which was quite dark, but by which we ascended to a small room, speedily filled by the whole town who could crowd within it. The Sheikh made his appearance; he was an old man, quite blind, and was led to his seat by a little boy. He proffered every facility to our proposed examination of the island, and seemed to feel a pleasure at the idea of again opening a communication with India. He was wretchedly poor, apparently with scarcely the necessaries of life; the only refreshment he could offer us was a few dates and some water. In our intercourse, through interpreters, with natives, we can never be too cautious. Thus the one we employed on this occasion purchased back, without my knowledge, for a few dollars, a very handsome case of pistols, worth about twenty-five pounds, the Sheikh being wholly ignorant of their value. We did not detect this for some weeks afterwards; and when we did, and the act was laid to his charge, he did not seem to think but that he had acted with perfect correctness.

## CHAPTER II.

Macullah first visited—its appearance from Seaward—its Houses—Amount of Population—Commerce—Somarelies—Banians—their love of gain—Attachment to and care of Bullocks—Slaves in Arabia—Expedition to enter Africans as Seamen—Visit Shaher—its Governor, Ali Ney—Ceremonies at the Feast of the Aids—Theft, how punished—Succession to the Government.

MACULLAH was not, I believe, known to the Portuguese navigators. In 1713, Thornton constructed a plan of its harbour; after which it was visited by several vessels. At present it serves as a coal depôt to the steam vessels of the East-India Company.

Approaching from seaward, a hill 600 feet in height, of a lighter colour than the rest of the mountain chain, rises close over the town, and forms an excellent mark for ascertaining its position; which from its being low, and of nearly the same colour as the coast, it might otherwise be difficult to do. Vessels anchor abreast the houses in fifteen fathoms water, about a quarter of a mile from the shore.

Macullah stands on a low projecting point, forming the northern extremity of a deep bay.

The houses are built close to the water's edge, but a ledge of rocks breaks the force of the swell, which in the south-west monsoon would otherwise overwhelm them. From seaward the houses have a lofty castellated appearance, the lower portion being constructed of stone, and the upper of sun-burnt bricks. Formerly the walls have been cemented over, but portions of this only now remain. At the upper part they are turreted, and they incline towards each other in the way observed in the towns of Upper Egypt. The windows are small, and mostly facing the sea. None of them are arched over, as those of Mocha and Jidda. Glass is not used; the doors are low, and the passages leading to the different apartments narrow and dark. The Governor's and the largest of these houses are constructed so as, if necessary, to stand a siege, and hence difficulties have been purposely thrown in the way of proceeding from one part to the other. A wall enclosing a circular space is even carried from the wall to the upper part of the house, so that those in possession of the lower part of the building could not deprive others at the upper of water.

What a state of society, where every man hourly expects to convert his house into a castle! Broils are of constant occurrence within the town, and the Bedowins not unfrequently attack it from without; so that from childhood to old age all are familiar with strife. A carpet, or mat, some cushions, and occasionally a rude couch, are their only furniture. The walls are duly decorated with the arms usually worn. A slave attends as junitor at the entrance of the Governor's house.

The population of Macullah is estimated at 7,000, who do not all reside within the town; the labourers, mariners, and poorer classes live in huts built on a sandy slope rising beyond the walls. At Mocha and Loheya the huts are remarkable for neatness of construction, but these are rude tenements raised from branches of the date's palm, and covered with coarse mats.

A range of blacksmiths' shops extends along the beach, behind which is the market. A wall extends on the eastern side, from the sea to the base of the mountains, and within the town there is a rude building mounting some old iron guns; while watch-towers have been erected on either side the valley leading to the interior.

The wells are situated in that direction, and the Bedowins, by taking possession of these, frequently reduce the inhabitants to great distress. In the rainy season a considerable stream fills the bed of this valley, which is not indeed at any season wholly dried up.

The sea-coast of Southern Arabia forms no exception to the wild sterility which characterizes other portions; but as we approach the ravines in the interior, or the mountain heights, we find the scene changed, and the eye is once more refreshed with traces of cultivation. Tobacco, indigo, wheat, and several other descriptions of grain, are reared in large quantities. The first is brought in bales, and five thousand, valued at fifty thousand dollars, are annually shipped to the African ports, and those in the lower portion of the Red Sea. The quantity of indigo there produced is also very considerable. Blue cloth, which is dyed here, is universally worn in this part of Arabia. A small quantity of indigo is also imported from the African coast.

Amidst the varied classes which are found in this town, the Soumalies, or natives of the opposite coast of Africa, are the most calculated to excite the attention of a stranger. Few reside here permanently, the greater number only remaining until their stock of sheep, gums, or coffee is disposed of. They are a remarkably fine race of men, and tall—their height varying from five feet nine inches to six feet two inches. They have well-knit limbs—a short or a corpulent person being rarely met with. Their skins are not very dark, though glossy, and appear to suffer from cutaneous disorders. Their features are mild, regular, and their expression pleasing.

A mutual hatred exists between the Arabs and this clsas—who do not, however, profess to dislike the English. A custom exists amidst this class, of changing the hair from its natural dark colour to a brown tinge, which they effect by plastering it with chumam. Not even children are exempted from this absurd custom. "Results and not processes are," we say, "for the public eye;" but with their craniums invested with a loading of this cement, Soumalies traverse the streets, regardless of such a maxim; They appear a bold generous race. The Arabs view them as Londoners would do rustics; however, as navigators the Soumalies are far superior to them, frequently crossing the Gulf of Aden when the Arabs are too timid to navigate along their own coast.

Southern Arabia is supplied with a vast number of sheep from Africa. They are of a very peculiar breed; the head is black, the fleece (if that which is more hair than wool deserve the appellation) is white, and the size far larger than any produced in Arabia. A fleshy appendage, similar to the dewlap of a cow, is observed in their necks. One to two dollars, according to the season, is the price paid for them. Whatever may be the duration of the voyage, which is generally three days, these animals are neither supplied with food nor water; yet, I never recollect seeing one which was not as fat as the generality of English sheep; but the fat has a different consistence and flavour, more nearly resembling tallow; otherwise the meat is nutritious and good.

In all the sea-port towns of Arabia we find a number of Indians called Banians, who arrive principally from Surat and Porebunder. To what privations will not men in the pursuit of gain subject themselves! For fifteen and twenty years, and often until age has wholly prevented them from enjoying the fruits of their industry, will this class remain in a foreign land, toiling on, wifeless and solitary; for neither their own prejudices nor Arab toleration will permit them either to marry or purchase female slaves. They are a meek, though persevering race, as superior to the Arabs in all appertaining to barter and commerce generally as one class ever will be to another. At the present time they have the greater portion of Arabian traffic in their hands. At Müscat, I knew a person of this cast, who, after remaining there until he had amassed a large fortune, died of old age on his return to and within sight of his native city. At Mocha, and some other towns in Yemen, they are subjected to many degradations; but not so here, where the Arabs permit them the free exercise of their religion, in all save the burning of their dead, compelling them in place thereof to inter the corpse in the ground. They buy up, and keep before their houses, a number of bullocks, feeding them with great care, and not unfrequently, when the animal continues in bad condition, shipping them off to India, consigning them there to the superior care of their brethren.

At the grain shops it is amusing to watch the assurance of these animals, who thrust their muzzles into every basket, taking a mouthful from each, the Banian merchant speaking to, and remonstrating, and quietly striving to put the animal's head on one side, but in vain; he tosses and shakes himself clear until he has levied his tax, and then proceeds to another shop. They well know the houses of their own masters from those of the Arabs, who do not display similar forbearance.

In Calcutta, and some other Indian towns, these animals have become very troublesome. It is customary there, when a rich Hindoo dies, to turn adrift, after the manner of the scape goat of the Israelites, a young bull, who thenceforth roams about, levying contributions in the manner which I have described, on the public. They are sleek and mischievous. Such a nuisance did they at one time become at this " City of Palaces," that they were all, by directions of the government, removed to the opposite side of the river. There they wandered like unquiet spirits, until some of their number ventured to enter the ferry boats, which are constantly plying. It would have been an impious act in the crew to have repulsed them, and all were therefore shortly found in their old quarters.

Our English seamen, when I was at Calcutta, had found a more effectual mode. It was discovered that the flesh of these pampered favourites was excellent, and many, nightly caught straying near the banks of the river, fell a sacrifice to our countrymen's taste for good beef.

For a town in this part of Arabia the trade of Macullah is considerable, and the Governor derives from a duty of four per cent. a revenue annually of 20,000 dollars. The port itself possesses few vessels, perhaps not more than twenty, but a great number touch here, on their route between India and the Red Sea. Dates, sulphur, and matchlocks arrive from Muscat; cottons, rice, and sugar from India; and occasionally a few slaves from the African coast. Indeed, with the exception of the mart at Mecca, where, during the pilgrimage, thousands are annually disposed of, there is less slaving in Arabia than perhaps any part of the East; and where it does exist the treatment which they receive is better than in many other parts of the world where they are called servants. They often take their meals with the family, are never beaten, nor spoken to with harshness, and if they are displeased with their master they can demand a public sale. Often too they rise to situations of great importance and trust. I have known instances where they have been entrusted with the command of most valuable ships; and their masters have related to me how implicitly in such cases they could rely on their judgment and good faith, as well as their superior skill in navigation.

I have myself frequently had occasion to observe that when the offspring of Africans, born either in Arabia or India, have received the advantage of an education, they fully justify these eulogiums. I cannot, therefore, help remarking here, how much it is to be regretted that greater encouragement is not held out for this class, to enter, in India, the Government service. Sir John Malcolm, at the suggestion of his brother, Admiral Sir Charles Malcolm, was induced, some years since, to direct one of their vessels of war to proceed to the African coast, for the purpose of bringing from thence as volunteers a number of youths, to serve in the vessels of the Indian navy. Difficulties had been experienced for some years in manning them with Indians, of which a portion of their crew consisted. It was represented that the Africans, a brave hardy race, would become after a short time scarcely inferior to Europeans; and as they were to receive a bounty on being received on board, and would serve under a branch of the British Legislature, it was thought no risk of violating the existing slave laws would be incurred in effecting this object. Sufficient care was not taken, however, on so very delicate a mission, to prevent this being done, for a decision of the Supreme Court of Bombay decided a recent Act to have been violated, and the boys thus entered were discharged; so that the project fell to the ground.

There can be no doubt but that the purchasing slaves for the purpose of manumitting them, is calculated to encourage the traffic. But both in India and in large Arabian towns, there are a number of negroes who have become free by the death of their masters. If these men or their sons could be induced to enter, we should effect an object which both policy and philanthropy render so desirable. With respect to their religious belief, all measures save those of persuasion or example (whatever the age of the lads be) would of necessity be avoided; but they so readily adopt the faith of their masters, that there is, I firmly believe, reason to think Christianity would receive more proselytes from these than any other class in the East.

The objects of the Government, in the expedition to which I have alluded, were evidently of the most benevolent description; trading in human flesh was never contemplated; and there yet appears no reason why, if such could be effected by taking free negroes and not slaves, volunteers should not be permitted to enter from Africa as from any other part of the world. A large proportion of all the vessels' crews within the Persian Gulf, Red Sea, and along the Indian coast, are of this class. Their muscular, and often gigantic forms, present a striking contrast to those of the Hindoos. That their courage is not inferior to their physical energies, has been often exhibited, in the sanguinary conflicts not long since of such frequent occurrence in these seas.

In this respect how remarkable is the change which a few years of British sway has effected! At the commencement of this century vessels dare not sail but in large numbers, and then most frequently under convoy. With the exception of Muscat, there were few other ports which did not openly encourage piratical pursuits. But now vessels trade from port to port alone, and without apprehension. It is a question if from a very early period this part of Arabia has enjoyed (if that may be called enjoyment which is a state of variance with the general habits of the people) a time more peaceful than at present.

From Macullah I took advantage of the absence of the vessel, which was not expected for some days, to journey to Shaher, which is situated to the eastward, and is the capital of a district of that name. I had heard much of the fame of its ruler, Ali Ney, and was not disappointed. Mocha presents the worst specimens of town Arabs, and Lord Valencia, in opposition to Niebhur, draws from those he was there in communication with, a very unfavourable description of them. Here, however, the middling and upper classes are very superior, more especially the sheikhs. Ali Ney would be considered a polished man in any society. Nor is the governor of Macullah in this respect inferior to him.

The former is a young man about thirty years of age, fair complexioned, of a tall figure, and somewhat of an exquisite in his dress and appearance, his fingers being tipped with henna, and his eye-lids with antimony. I received much attention and civility from him during my stay in the town, which is one of the largest on this coast, extending, at its greatest length, one mile and a half. A great many mosques are found here; they are very rude buildings, usually surrounded with a colonnade of pointed arches.

The people of this and other towns in Southern Arabia differ greatly from those in the more northern parts of the Peninsula; the upper classes are mostly from the hill districts, very fair, with features partaking of a Jewish cast;

they are fond of maritime pursuits, and their sailors bear the reputation of being the best on the coast.

The feast of the Aid (instituted in commemoration of God staying the hand of Abraham) occurred during my stay, and their usual dress of a shirt—a cloth reaching only to the knee, leaving the leg bare, and confined to their waist with a leathern girdle—was exchanged for the richest they could procure. Those colours are usually chosen which are the most gorgeous, and form the strongest contrast to each other, such as scarlet, yellow, or purple. One of my boatmen, whose pay during the year was not twenty dollars, appeared in a turban worth twice that sum.

Females here wear a very peculiar veil, which is pierced with four or more square openings, bordered with silver or gold lace. Several of these damsels are heavily burthened with silver finery; on a girl about sixteen I have counted fifty earrings, (they suspend them one within the other) besides tubes or cylinders, some three inches in length, fastened about the forehead and neck. With a preparation from India they dye their faces with a number of lines, stars, and other figures. Men assembled in groups, exercising themselves in feigned combat with their long swords, or amusing themselves in paying and receiving visits.

It is singular that we found no coffee-houses in this town, but each person, not excepting the governor, on such occasions carries with him the necessary quantity in a small basket. Crimes otherwise than those incidental to frequent broils, appear of rare occurrence with these people; and merchandize is openly exposed without any fear of the pilferer. Mutilation, if the crime is aggravated, is the punishment for theft; if otherwise, the head of the offender is shaved, he is placed on an ass, and, after being subjected to the derision of the people, is punished by stripes and imprisonment.

I visited the prison, a square tower, the walls about thirty feet in height. Some prisoners were within, manacled both by their hands and legs; their offence was robbery, and forty dollars was fixed as the price of their release. Their fare on such occasions consists of coarse millet, bread, and water; yet were they laughing, and apparently in the best of spirits. Justice in every case is administered by the *dowlah* or governor in person. His decisions are brief, and there is no appeal from them.

Several Bedowins, during my stay, arrived from the interior, bringing cases for the arbitration of Ali Ney—a high opinion being entertained throughout the country of his judgment and probity. They were only acquainted with Europeans or their customs through the report of their merchants. I was probably the first Englishman who in the memory of the oldest inhabitant had landed there.

The rule which is exercised by the governors of these towns is mild and tolerant. Nominally, hereditary succession is looked to, but in almost every case it is disputed by the various branches of the family. He who by money can command the services of the greater number of Bedowins is usually the successful candidate. At Macullah, a few years since, when the old governor died, there was fighting in the town for a week ere the matter was decided.

From Shaher I must conduct my reader to Aden. There is little in the intermediate coast to interest him. The Bay of Broon, situated under a dark lofty promontory, forming the western horn of the bay of Macullah, is one of the few harbours which afford any protection to shipping during the south-west monsoon. Native boats and vessels which are unable from the lateness of the season to effect a passage, run in and remain here; there are no dangers. A small village, erected at the gorge of a pass, is occupied by about 500 inhabitants. It is similar in its features to Muscat Cove. The heat is as great as it is there, and though this ripens their dates, yet it in the same degree subjects them to violent and dangerous fevers. Water is very plentiful and good. I was very forcibly struck with the general resemblance of the face of the country to that of Socotra.

The Diebay Bedowins, who occupy a large portion of the intermediate coast between this cape and Aden, have some peculiarities; they have no head sheikh, but are split into seven sections, each having a chief, and those meet together whenever its affairs require it, to consult on the general interests of the tribe. Their number is estimated at 8,000 matchlocks, and they are considered amidst the wildest and most ferocious tribes in Yemen. Strangers dare not land within the line of their territories. I made an attempt to do so, but before the boat could approach the shore they were seen clustering in every hillock, and as my object was merely to obtain the latitude, I did not persevere, much to the satisfaction of the Arab boatmen with me, who, though we were well armed, by no means relished an encounter with these tribes.

At Mughadain, on this part of the coast, I observed a most remarkable difference in the amount of magnetic variation. At Bombay it is scarcely perceptible, and proceeding along this coast to the westward, it gradually and proportionably increases, until within a full mile of this, to five degrees twenty minutes westerly, but here it decreased to four degrees forty-six minutes. I was never so puzzled; I had two theodolites and a small azimuth compass, and all gave the same results. Thinking there might be local attraction, I tried several parts of the beach, and then removed far from rocks, to an open sandy space, and still the amount was the same. Quitting this, and advancing to the eastward, in a few miles it again resumed its progressive increase without interruption.

To what are we to attribute this deflection? Can it be that we here hit on some point where the variation line makes an abrupt and unusual turn? Has a similar "fault" been observed in any other part of the world? The dip I observed on the same occasion to be very great, one end of the magnetic needle being nearly lifted above the platina rim of the theodolite.

Whenever the navigator can land he will find this instrument the best adapted for ascertaining the amount of magnetic variation. It is merely necessary to defend the eye (should the instrument not be provided with it) by a coloured lens. The altitude and bearing are thus obtained together, and but one observer is required.

## CHAPTER IX.

Approach Cape Aden—Strength of Fortifications—Jews—Author proceeds to Lahesdj—Caravan Assembles—Docility and Fleetness of Camels—Arrives at the Sultan's Palace—Bedowins attack the City—Appearance of the Coast between Aden and Shaher—Natural Divisions of Arabia—Jaffa and Hydramout—North-east Monsoon, its duration and influence—Erroneous position assigned to the Bay of Hargiah—Islands off the Coast—Tides.

WITH a noble breeze we rapidly approached Cape Aden. Dark frowning masses of clouds capped the summit of its lofty peaks, heavy rains fell occasionally, and the landscape wore a gloomy aspect; but as we neared the shore, the day brightened, exposing the varied tints and singular stratification of this remarkable group. It compases an isolated mass of pinnacled hills, situated on a low sandy promontory, and on this account, as we approached from seaward, resembled an island.

From the earliest period Aden has been considered valuable as a naval station, and when the Turks possessed Yemen they fortified it with immense labour. An enormous wall has been carried completely over the whole range of mountains, and on one of the loftiest peaks they even contrived to place a long brass gun, seventeen feet in length, turning on a swivel.

Aden naturally is, perhaps, one of the strongest places in the world. From the land it can only be approached along the isthmus which I have mentioned, and thence but by one steep and narrow pass; while from seaward, Gibraltar does not expose a more formidable front. Very recently the British, with a view to its establishment as a coal depôt, failing to negociate for its purchase, despatched a force, and, with little opposition, possessed themselves of it. Some hopes, I believe, were entertained that the coffee trade, which now finds its way to the Red Sea by the ports of Mocha and Hoderda, might, under a settled form of government, be diverted to this channel, and that consequently we should possess a more direct control and participation in that important branch of Arabian commerce, which has so long been the project of the wise ruler of Egyptian affairs.

There is little now to denote the former magnificence and opulence of Aden; a few minarets, tottering to their fall, rear themselves above a score of wretched houses, and some miserable huts tenanted by Arabs, Banians, and Jews, not exceeding eight hundred or a thousand souls. A wall, now in ruins, formerly surrounded them. The Turkish cemetery, containing still some turbaned pillars of fine marble, extends from the level of the wall to the mosque of Sheikh Egdreese, which contains the remains of the holy man whose name it bears. This edifice is much revered by the Arabs, and other Mahomedans.

The Jews which are found here and in other parts of Yemen retain, in a striking degree, all the characteristics of their race; they distil and retail ardent spirits, and otherwise employ themselves in working gold and silver ornaments. They are fair, and many of their children remarkably pretty; we are surprised, amidst such a scene of wretchedness, to view their bright sunny cheeks, their coral lips, and sparkling eyes. By the Arabs they are treated with little consideration, and I have seen an urchin, pulling the beard of an aged Jew and spitting in his face, receive encouragement from the bystanders.

At the period I had been despatched to Aden for the purpose of making observations along the line of our survey, during the time I remained for that purpose I received an invitation to proceed with a caravan to the town of Lahesdj, the capital of a maritime district, and the residence of its ruler, Sultan Mahassan. He had quarrelled with some of the neighbouring tribes who now infested the intermediate country, and it was not judged safe to proceed until three hundred and fifty camels had assembled. A party of Jews, mounted on asses, attempted to join the party, but were at first driven away with blows and reproaches, but the leader afterwards permitted them, by each paying half a dollar, to follow in the rear.

All was now arranged, and on the 15th of March, 1834, the caravan was put in motion. Following along a broad valley, we arrived at the pass, which is about a mile from the town. The rocks on either hand present a great diversity of colouring; vertical bands of red, purple, or yellow, have a singular appearance where the rocks are otherwise of the darkest hue. The pass, being too narrow to admit of more than one camel at a time, has been widened by art. A square tower was built over its extremity, where we found, in passing through the gates, a few soldiers, black as negroes, quietly lounging and smoking their pipes. They did not condescend to take any notice of myself or my companions, although our garb must have pointed us out as strangers. Emerging from this pass, we obtained a view of the other harbour of Aden, called Back Bay; the waters of which were quite tranquil, and it had the appearance of a vast lake studded with rocky islets.

I turned aside from the caravan to visit the grave of a brother officer, who had a few weeks before been buried here; a heap of stones to protect the corpse from wild beasts, was the only token to mark the spot where our gallant companion was laid. I know few things more calculated to inspire mournful feelings, than to thus find a fellow voyager and countryman cut off in the prime of life, and his remains forming, on a silent unpeopled shore, a single solitary mound. Such a feeling we can imagine would, though to a greater degree, enter the breast of an African traveller, who, amidst the burning desert, should bend over a similar sad memorial of some bold adventurer, who, in the cause of science, had thus prematurely perished. Lieut. Pinching was attached to a surveying vessel, and fell a victim in the prime of life, deservedly regretted, to his zeal for the furtherance of the objects of the expedition.

The isthmus which connects Aden with the main is not more than a hundred yards in width, and across it a wall has been thrown; beyond this barrier a paved road extends to within a short distance of Lahesdj. It was a work of great labour, for the lower portion was laid with burnt bricks, and then covered with a concrete, nearly a foot in thickness, of sand, lime and pebbles; time has only had the effect of increasing its hardness and solidity. The present seems to be the age of road-making experiments. Would one thus constructed be worth the trial?

It was the high road to Sana, of which Aden was formerly the port, and the communication must have been very great to have caused the Turks to have built it. The country before us was a level marshy track. We crossed, by means of rude bridges, several streams of salt water, which flowed some distance into the interior, and then entered on an extensive plain. Apprehensions of the Futhali Bedowins kept our party on the alert.

I have never in Arabia seen more magnificent camels than those on which we were now mounted; in those parts of which the foregoing part of these volumes treat, and in Egypt, their pace, at speed, is a shuffling trot, rarely exceeding six or eight miles an hour; but the camels of Yemen carry their heads erect, throw out their legs with as much freedom and boldness as a horse, and their progress, at what appears their natural pace, cannot be less than twelve or fourteen miles an hour; the rider sits too in a peculiar manner, with the foot placed on the neck, and the body resting on the animal's shoulders; with the former, he urges the animal to speed. It was very animating to see our guards ride off at full speed, in groups of ten or a dozen, to scour the country, their long hair streaming behind them, and their animals, by means of a nose-ring, turning, stopping, and being kept under as complete command as a horse. Now they all discharge their muskets in the air, and, wheeling round again, approach in a line, chaunting their war-song, and flourishing their formidable swords.

About eight miles from Aden we halted at the tomb of Sheikh Osman, where there is also a small mosque and well of water. This edifice it formed by a double line of small cupolas, within an oblong coffin of ornamented woodwork, raised about three feet from the ground; it is covered with red cloth, the floor is matted, and a few silver lamps, together with ostrich eggs and other votive offerings, are suspended from the ceiling. Our guides very devoutly prayed over these, and concluded their devotions by feigning to collect dust from the cloth to heap on their heads.

The country now quite alters its character. In place of the low land and swampy tract we had quitted, we entered amidst sand downs, twenty or thirty feet in height, and covered with bushes and trees. All these several trees are said to produce gum. We halted beyond the skirts of the town shortly after dark, where we dismounted and walked to the palace. We found ourselves before a huge gate, at which we knocked, and were admitted by a small wicket into a spacious hall, dimly lighted, and nearly filled with armed Bedowins. Spears, shields, swords, and other weapons, crowded the walls; there was a fire burning, to which we drew near; all were loudly talking, when we entered, but there was now a general silence; in this part of Arabia it is not etiquette to address questions until the stranger has been presented to their chief.

In about ten minutes a slave appeared and beckoned us to follow him, which we did, through an immense number of spacious apartments and narrow passages, till we reached a small room in one corner of the building. There we found the sultan, a dirty, mean, corpulent man, about fifty years of age, reclining lazily on a cushion. Two chairs in the middle of the apartment were placed for us, pipes and coffee brought, and a few compliments exchanged, and the sultan welcomed us in brief phrase to his dwelling and his country. The apartment into which we were shown, probably the smallest in the palace, not being more than fourteen feet square, was lighted by rude lamps suspended from the ceiling, and four slaves stood at either corner with wax tapers in their hands; on the floor were seated several Bedowin Sheikhs; in one corner stood an old time-piece, presented at some former period to our host by the British Government; several recesses were occupied by copper dishes and earthenware.

A meal had been prepared for us in another room, consisting of fried pancakes, lumps of grilled meat, melted ghee, and huge dishes of rice. Another of rather coarser fare had also been provided for our guides.

After taking leave of the sultan, we quitted the palace for a house in the town which had been prepared for us. Our host was an intelligent old man, and entertained us to a late hour with stories of the English, who had, in 1801, under Colonel Murray, been stationed at Aden. At this period there was an impression that our Government was again likely to occupy that town, and I believe our host spoke the sentiments of his countrymen in general when he expressed a strong desire that this should take place. Individually, their coldness and reserve may render my countrymen not always agreeable to the natives of the East, but every where are they for other qualities respected; their probity is highly extolled, and for justice, our Government enjoys an equal reputation.

A lively recollection is preserved there of the excesses of the Turks during their stay in Yemen, and that race is every where spoken of with abhorrence.

We found the sultan, when we visited him on the morrow, desirous to obtain our aid to act against his neighbours the Futhalee Bedowins, who at the present moment were pressing him very hard. I could hold out to him no such hopes, but promised to forward his application to my superiors. He produced a treaty, which his father had entered into with Sir Home Popham, at the time he visited the Red Sea, by which, on the fulfilment of certain conditions respecting the occupation of Aden, we bound ourselves to assist him. The French were at this time in Egypt, and Sir Home then could hardly have contemplated that we should again require the same port as a depôt, to carry on that extensive scheme of steam-navigation which will be very shortly established between the eastern and western world.

Lord Valentia gives a high character of Ahmed Sultan Mahussan's predecessor, describing him as the bravest and most polite of the chiefs of Yemen. He encouraged commercial pursuits amidst his subjects, coveted the sojourn of foreigners in his dominions, and was liberal and just in all his decisions.

Had his successor followed his example, Aden would ere this have recovered some portion of its former commercial importance; for, whether to receive the products of India, those of Africa, or the commerce of the west, it is most advantageously situated, and will, I have little doubt, ere long again arise from its ruins.

Ahmed amassed considerable treasure, which his successor strove to increase by arbitrary exactions; but the merchants fled, and the greater portion has been wasted in purchasing the aid of one neighbouring wild tribe to protect him against the incursions of others.

There is a curious custom existing here, which also tended to lighten his coffers. The principal rulers in Yemen are expected to send a considerable sum annually to the several smaller states as a present, and if this is withheld the party consider they have a fair right to rob and agitate until it is given. This led to the present rupture with the Futhalee Bedowins, who had now infested the town.

On one occasion, during our stay, they effected an entry at night, burnt several houses, and, without interruption, carried off a considerable booty. A day or two afterwards they encountered a small party journeying to Aden, when they slew some soldiers of the caravan, stripping and otherwise maltreating the remainder. We buried their bodies on our return.

With a due regard to our safety, a guard was stationed at the house where we lodged. At night they were not agreeable tenants, for they beguiled the whole period of their watch with songs; and when one party, becoming hoarse or tired, gave us hope of rest, they were succeeded by another, who commenced with double vigour. Nor were these the only noises which broke the silence of night. All those stationed to look out around the walls of the town, keep up a perpetual shouting, to let it be known they are on the alert. The effect of this in certain parts of the world, as in Muscat, when the voice of the solitary watcher rises clear and sonorous, and is echoed by another from afar, is very pleasing; but here such cries were mingled with the roaring of camels, the yelling of old women, the barking of dogs, crying of children, and continued throughout the whole of the night.

Here for a week were we doomed to remain, for there was no caravan in readiness to proceed, and the sultan would not listen to our proposal of journeying with a small guard, which was all I solicited.

I have little to say of Lahesdj. It occupies a large space, but its inhabitants do not exceed 5,000. The palace of the governor is an extensive and lofty building, and there are several large private houses; but in general the inhabitants are lodged in huts of a conical form, and rudely constructed from the straw of millet. Within the walls large spaces are appropriated to the reception of filth and rubbish, which is heaped up in mounds; the same may be observed outside Egyptian towns.

Markets are held here on Tuesdays and Thursdays, when the Bedowins exchange their butter, frankincense, and cattle, for grain and cloths. The bazaar is well supplied with these several articles.

The females manufacture a coarse cloth here,

and there are several establishments of silk weavers. The colour of the yarn which is received in India is good, but their devices here are rude and their workmanship coarse. The inhabitants of this and other towns along this coast are of the Zeydee sect, the tenets of which admit of the exercise of more liberality to those of another faith than the several other scions of Mahomedanism.

We had nothing to do but to receive and pay visits. A sumptuous meal was sent us every day from the sultan's table, and our host was unremitting in his attentions. Still the time passed but heavily, and I was not sorry when the period arrived for us to leave. To enliven our stay a number of dancing girls were introduced. Their performance does not differ from that of the Almahs of Egypt, and I was surprised to hear that the Arabs do not at marriages scruple to admit them. One of the sheikh's sons was a constant visitor of ours; he was an intelligent lad, about twenty, and had made the journey several times to Sanaa and its neighbourhood, and spoke with enthusiasm on the richness of the intermediate country.

The haft of this young man's dagger was studded with gold coins; he had nothing else in his costume different from others in the town.

Daggers usually worn here have a cumbrous ornament attached to the end of their sheaths, and rising from where the dagger is in their girdle, to nearly the height of the wearer's chin. A large powder-horn, studded with brass, is carried alongside of it.

The powder used by the Arabs is very coarse grained, and in firing, a third does not ignite; and the length of their cartridge, if he were not apprised of this, would therefore astonish an European. Whenever English powder is given to these people, care should be taken to explain its relative strength, as by neglecting to do so I have seen more than one accident occur.

Ground is cultivated to a great extent in the vicinity of Lahesdj, and to a yet greater, it was described to me, as the traveller advances towards the interior. On the eighth day after our arrival a guard was collected, and I returned to Aden.

The following remarks may give some idea of the physical geography of these regions, although they possess little of interest, for the whole sea-coast varies but in a trifling degree. We have every where the same mountain range, nearly, in fact, encircling the whole continent; the same intermediate plain, inhabited by tribes, differing little but in a greater degree of wildness and ferocity; occasionally a fertile valley, as that of Meifah, in which I found the ruins of Nukub el Hedger. That of Hawhar, leading to the town of the same name, and some other cultivated portion similar to that which I have just quitted, entirely owe their fertility to mountain streams, which in the rainy season fill their beds and reach the sea. From the hills they bring but little fertilizing principle; yet the soil, of a hard clay, aided by a powerful sun, when well watered, is very productive, especially where the upper stratum from time becomes formed of decayed vegetation. The ground is carefully freed from stones, and portioned out into small patches, separated from each other by narrow embankments, serving a double purpose of holding the rain for some time after it has fallen, and for forming the upper part of the ridge into channels.

Their implements of husbandry are the same as those which will be found figured and well described by Niebhur. The plough, which is drawn by two oxen, merely scratches without turning over the ground, and their only harrow is a bush, which is drawn over the surface.

Barley, in productive seasons, yields two crops, the one before, and the other after the south-west monsoon. Water melons, plantains, cocoa-nuts, limes, mangoes, and most of our culinary vegetables, are reared in considerable quantities. Few flowers are cultivated; but we have, among other odoriferous plants, the Arabian jessamine, reared for the sake of its perfume, and highly valued by the Arabian females. The shrub grows with much luxuriance, yet the scent seems less powerful than that we have in India.

Senna grows wild on the plains, and, independent of its other properties, the Arabs consider it valuable in their treatment of wounds and cuts.

The general elevation of the mountain chain between Aden and Shaher is from three to five thousand feet, its highest points rising over Shougre and Mughadane. It is of limestone formation, and presents the usual characteristics of that rock. The secondary ranges exhibit a greater diversity of form and outline, as well as of colour; sometimes of a dark red or green, but more generally of a jet black, contrasting in a remarkable manner with the glistening white sand which sometimes rises on an unbroken plain seven or eight hundred feet, filling up the valleys, and adding to the ruggedness of an outline produced by masses of volcanic rock strewn about in great confusion. So numerous are these masses, that as they lay piled in heaps the one on the other, they may readily be taken for mounds of ruins.

Coffee, frankincense, aloes, and dragon's-blood, are the principal products of the mountain range; the latter is produced not many miles to the eastward of Shougre. There are two kinds of frankincense: meaty, which is the most valuable, sells at about four dollars the hundred-weight, and is chewed by the Arabs to sweeten their breath; the other, an inferior kind, is disposed of at about twenty per cent. less. Both the Arabian aloe and the dragon's-blood are the same as those which will be found at Socotra.

The natural divisions of Arabia are probably more distinctly marked than those of most other countries; but modern geographers, by adopting the arbitrary divisions of the Greeks and Romans, or the contradictory statements of the earlier Oriental geographers, have created much confusion. The division of the former into "the Desert," "the Stony," and "the Happy," was not more inapplicable to the whole Peninsula, than are now the various other divisions into which the latter authorities have portioned it. D'Anville was compelled to acknowledge that it was scarcely possible to fix precisely the limits of each Arabian province.

Burckhardt, during his stay at Hedjaz, found that the designation of that province was applied by the natives of the country to but a small portion of the space it occupies on our maps; and I may observe the same of the two great provinces of Djaffa and Hydramaut, the coast of which has hitherto been considered the southern boundary.

That the earlier Arabian writers were justified, at the period they wrote, in fixing the boundaries of these divisions, I imagine there can be but little doubt, since the traditions of the inhabitants bear evidence to the whole of this part of the country (which has been ever, and is still, changing its mastery) having been subjected to these provinces. But as these have now shrunk to their present limits, it has seemed to me desirable that they should be characterized as they are now known to the natives of the country; and whenever, in the course of the following pages, their names occur, they have no more extended signification than is here mentioned.

By Djaffa, the Arabs designate the whole of the mountains, from the territories of the

Theshed e Bekyl east as far as the coffee is grown; which would be a line taken north about twenty miles to the eastward of Shougre. By Hydramaut, they include only an extensive and fertile valley about sixty miles in length, running nearly parallel to the sea-coast, and situated four days' travelling on foot from Macullah, and four and a half from Shaher. Beyond this approximation I have no means of fixing either of its extremities.

The coast between Aden and Shaher is occasionally broken by bays, of which the largest are those of Macullah and Goobut-Ain; but beyond a small cove at Ras Broom, and an anchorage formed by the small island near to Hassan Ghorab, there are no harbours which afford shelter in the south-west monsoon.

A capacious bay thickly studded with islets appears in most modern charts of this part of the coast of Arabia, under the designation of the bay of Hargeah. Now, two days' distant from Hassan Gorab, there is a town called Hargeah, from whence the coast may have received its name; but it is very certain, from our researches, that the bay here referred to has no existence.

The chart between Ras Kubb and Ras Ruttull exhibits but a slight indentation; and a line drawn from both these points leaves the large island without it. Some small rocky islets nearer the shore may have possibly led to this mistake. The largest of the group, Burragha, lies off Ras Mugdah, from which it is separated by a narrow channel about three hundred yards in width. It is composed of gritstone and sandstone, which is twisted and distorted in a most extraordinary manner. The highest of its points was ascertained to be eight hundred feet. A smaller island, called by the Arabs Skab, or Gibboose, from its resemblance to an Arab guitar, lies within a short distance of Burragha. It swells to a rounded hump at one extremity, from which a piece of table-land from seaward apparently extends to the other; but it was found, on landing, to be nearly divided into two portions, and a low narrow slip alone connects them.

A chain of rocky islets, extending about three-quarters of a mile from the shore, lies off Maghadain, but the coast is otherwise free from islands and dangers. A broad bank of soundings extends the whole distance; the bottom is either mud or sand; coral reefs are not met with. The depth in general is a sufficient indication of an approach to the shore. The north-east monsoon blows along this coast; and between these points there is, in consequence, but little surf; to the eastward of Macullah it is very high. There is very little tide on this coast: the flood sets to the eastward, at a velocity of two and a half miles an hour; but the strong currents I have before mentioned frequently interfere with and alter the set of the tides.

## CHAPTER IV.

Arrive at Socotra—Its appearance—Contradictory descriptions—Tamarida—Its Houses—Cemeteries—Suspicion of its Inhabitants—Quit the Town—Perilous pass—Camels—Cadhoop—Caverns serving as Habitations—Face of the Country—Process of making Knives—Tanning Skins—Inscriptions—Resemblance to the early Ethiopic—A Steamer passes—Socotrean Marriage—Amusements—Slaves.

I NOW quit Arabia and proceed to the Island of Socotra. Considering their magnitude and the position they occupy, it appears singular we should know so little either of Madagascar or this island. The former, however, is considered to be so insalubrious that no European could remain there; nor did the reports we heard from the Arabs induce us to suppose we should find Socotra much less so.

The day was clear and bright when we made the land, and steering for Tamarida, the principal town, we were soon at anchor within the bay. As compared with the unwooded and barren appearance of the coast we had quitted, the prospect before us was singular. A range of granite mountains rose near the beach, terminating in pointed spires, grey or red. These summits offered a curious contrast to the green and umbrageous foliages with which the lower portions were clothed. Some rain had evidently very recently fallen, for the whole looked fresh and lively, and some sparkling cascades gleamed forth in the sun's rays.

This island appears to have been known at an early period to the ancient geographers: Ptolemy notices it under the appellation of Dioscorides Insula; and Arrian says that the inhabitants of it were subject, as they are now, to the kings of the Incense country. For a very long period it appears to have attracted little attention, and may almost be considered as lost to geographers until the visit of Marco Polo in the thirteenth century, who does not, however, make any particular mention of its inhabitants and resources. Vasco de Gama, in his memorable voyage from Lisbon to Calicut, in 1497, passed without seeing it; seven years afterwards it was made known to European navigators by Fernandez Perara; and Albuquerque at a somewhat later period took possession of it. At the commencement of the seventeenth century, when the increasing spirit of commerce and enterprize led several of our squadrons to enter the ports in the Red Sea, it was frequently visited for shelter or refreshment; and in 1800, when the French army was in Egypt, Commodore Blanket was authorized to take possession of it, but does not appear to have found this necessary or advisable under the circumstances in which he was placed.

It is most amusing to observe in what varied terms those several visitors describe the island. Captain Dawnton says that its chief produce is aloes, though the annual amount does not exceed a ton; that cattle may be bought, but are exceedingly small; that according to the dry rocky barrenness of the island, wood is at twelvepence a man's burthen, and every other particular is very dear; concluding that the whole island is composed of stones, arid and bare. Another authority says, "It is a populous, fruitful island," &c.

Yet both those writers may have described appearances as they presented themselves. There is evidence to prove that the island was formerly more productive than at present; such parts moreover as are exposed to the view of the passing traveller are mostly limestone cliffs, of which some portions are, indeed, covered with a scanty sprinkling of soil, but generally of an inferior quality, and so hard that the grass which it occasionally nourishes dries up, almost as soon as the rain ceases which may have caused it to spring forth.

I pass over the various difficulties which I encountered in obtaining camels, &c. for my examination of the interior of the island, a duty which was assigned to me, while the commander examined the sea-shore. I was highly pleased with this arrangement, and my preparations were soon made; a small tent, the requisite instruments, and a few presents, were all with which I encumbered myself. My companions were Mr. Cruttenden, midshipman, and John Sunday, a Nubian boy.

Tamarida offers little to interest the reader. It has been of greater extent, but the Wahabees, in 1801, paid a visit to, and destroyed it. The houses are now more numerous than the inhabitants, and the cemeteries are awfully extensive, fully confirming that which we had previously heard of the extraordinary insalubrity of the climate. A semicircle of hills encloses a space about four miles in width, and watered by three streams; one of these flows past the town, which is situated on the sea-shore, about midway between the two capes. The water is light and good, and whalers occasionally touch here, to fill up with that necessary.

Here, and in some parts of the Arabian

coast, the houses are built of coral. From its softness this is easily hewn into the required shape, and is every where found in great abundance. To prevent the rapid decay of these edifices from the action of the rain, they are cemented over. The process of calcination is very simple; they first dig a hollow in the sand, cover it with firewood, and place the coral, broken into small fragments, over it; a fire is then lighted, and as the lime is produced it falls into the hollow; sand is added to this when mortar is required, and its durability and adhesiveness is then very great. Few of the houses here are more than two stories in height; the upper portion being considered the harem, and the lower being used for the transaction of business. To each a neat garden is attached, in which are grown some tobacco and a few vegetables.

It may serve to show the primitive simplicity of the people amidst whom I found myself, when I state that the only authority to which the natives could refer me for furtherance of my views was an old man, an Arab, named Abdallah, who had been formerly a sepoy in the service of an Indian prince. There were no sheikhs nor governor; every one pursues uninterruptedly his own avocations, nor seems to care for those of his neighbours.

From our first arrival, the natives, supposing the vessel to be a whaler, flocked down from the hills, bringing aloes and dragon's blood to exchange for dates, grain, tobacco, &c. In these transactions money is rarely used, certain quantities of *ghee,** or fragments of amber and ambergris, being substituted. The principal object for which they covet dollars is to convert them into earrings and other ornaments for their women.

Abdallah received me in a filthy apartment, about eight feet long and six broad. The Sultan of Kisseen's letter he coolly and unhesitatingly pronounced to be a forgery of our own, and this opinion he maintained until some presents induced him to change it. It was vexing, yet amusing, to hear the various speculations with which this people indulged as to the real object of our visit; it was certainly either to look for gold, or to examine the island prior to taking possession.

It will be remembered by those who have perused an account of the early voyages and operations of the Portuguese in the East, that the peculiar advantages of position enjoyed by

* Clarified butter.

Socotra were not overlooked by that adventurous nation, and under their illustrious Albuquerque, after a noble resistance from the Arabs, they possessed themselves of two forts in the vicinity of Tamarida. Of these they retained possession for some months, but they were eventually, from the insalubrity of the climate, compelled to evacuate them. There is now nothing to denote their visit, excepting some singular tales preserved by the natives, and occasional fragments of their armour, which are found near to the forts, the ruins of which still remain.

On the 13th January 1834, my difficulties were surmounted; I was furnished with camels, and told that I was at liberty to proceed in any direction I wished.

I could not but remark the singular mode in which our baggage was placed; instead of allowing it to be suspended on each side, as is customary in Egypt and Arabia, they pile a succession of thick hair mats over the hump and along the back, which they bind up by cords into a ridge, and then stow the several articles in long baskets on either side; on the top of these were placed our beds, serving us, at an elevation of thirteen feet from the ground, as saddles.

Thus, amidst the adieus of the inhabitants,

we quitted Tamarida, to proceed on our tour. My object this evening was merely to get without the town, and clear of its inhabitants, whose curiosity from the first was unbounded, leaving us with scarcely a minute to ourselves. The change to an open and pure atmosphere was also most pleasing. Hamed, our guide, was an intelligent active man, very inquisitive withal, especially as regards our religious observances. Our neglect of morning and evening adoration had attracted his attention, nor could he be made to understand that those would pray in private who did not do so in public.

January 14th. We struck our tent, and were journeying before sunrise. Crossing a plain thickly covered with bushes, we found the path led along the cliffs which bound the shore. Those accustomed to see the camel only in the desert, would be surprised at the facility, provided the surface be rough, with which this animal will traverse mountain tracts; but our poor creatures were sorely tried here, the road leading across some rounded and smooth limestone-rocks, over which we could not, without the aid of our hands, contrive to scramble. Having accomplished this, I turned to watch the progress of our camels. Three crossed in safety, but the fourth slipped at the worst part of the pass, and slid down the rock for some distance; but by inserting the joint of his hinder leg into a hollow, he cautiously contrived to regain his footing. A few feet more and he would have rolled over the precipice and been dashed to pieces. The movements of any other animal would most probably, by fright, have hastened its own destruction.

The natives here, Arab-like, have built up, with much labour, certain portions of the path, but have left the worst, as if in despair, wholly untouched. From the range which rises above us, very large masses have been detached, some of which appear just arrested, in the act of rushing down the steep; the weight or impetus of others have overcome every obstacle, and lie strewn in enormous masses along the coast. One of these, forming a bold promontory, was not less than two hundred feet high.

I once, at a subsequent period, had barely passed the same spot, when my attention was arrested by a low, rumbling noise behind me. I turned instantly, and, to my great astonishment, saw one of these huge masses but just separated from the body of the hill. Its first course was but slow, though down a slope; its velocity however quickly increased, a short projection caught the base, and over toppled the whole hill—for so I may, from its magnitude, term it. The crashing which immediately succeeded was terrific, but a cloud of dust arose, and I could no longer trace its headlong career; the effects, however, were apparent enough, as soon as the dust cleared away; for a shock, like that of an earthquake, announced that the main body had reached the sea. A wave rose slowly and heavily along the coast, but in a few minutes all had again subsided.

To continue my journey. A heavy gale had prevailed for some hours on the previous night, and even now it blew hard; the sea rolled, chafed, and foamed, amidst the rocks below, with a noise that, even at the height of two hundred feet, was almost deafening. The action of the waves had worn the cliffs into subterraneous hollows, and it was curious to observe how these, as they became filled, threw forth, from orifices in the upper part, the water which tumbled headlong into them.

Two hours' brisk walking brought me to a pass, at the foot of which the plain again commenced, and from this we saw the small and pretty looking village of Cadhoop, situated on a sandy promontory; the white walls of its houses showing in strong outline against the dark foliage of the date trees which lie beyond it.

A few fishing boats dotted the surface of a deep lagoon, which nearly encompasses the hamlet, and a native vessel in the offing was about to approach the beach, where several persons had assembled to greet her crew. Below, we entered a date grove, watered by numerous streams, and then through a path which led to the village, where we pitched our tent.

To avoid numerous visitors, and to obtain a better and purer air, (for that of the village was damp and unhealthy,) I moved on the following morning to the base of the hill. The villagers were too lazy to follow me, and I passed a few days very agreeably, in sketching, and wandering over the country.

The spot where we had encamped was elevated and dry, and the mountain breezes swept keen and fresh down the vallies. Several herds of cows, and numerous flocks of sheep or goats, were feeding on the luxuriant herbage and the numerous aromatic plants which grew in great great profusion around.

Various were the adventures which we met with during these excursions. Mr. Cruttenden was an invaluable ally to me. He spoke the Arabic language far better than myself; was always good-humoured and cheerful; and entered, with a midshipman's love of frolic, into all which our present mode of life brought before us. Our day's labour was usually terminated about sunset; Sunday by that time had prepared our evening meal, and as we talked of the affairs of the day over a cheerful fire, we could not avoid contrasting our present mode of life with that to which sailors in a tropical climate are subjected while cooped up on ship-board, especially in a small vessel.

To balance against what are usually called comforts, and the absence of which are perhaps necessary to give to the true traveller his natural tone of enjoyment, we were in nowise hurried as to time, and could consequently halt in those places which, like the present, we found the most pleasing. The climate too, appeared cool and salubrious, and we, in a word, had all which could make our tour at once pleasing and interesting.

On one of these excursions, I scaled the almost perpendicular face of a hill, to the distance of about seven hundred feet. The ascent continued for about two-thirds the height, in a gentle slope, covered with vegetation and trees; beyond that the limestone cliffs exposed a grey weather-beaten appearance, and numerous caves and hollows. These are used by the natives as habitations; for in a humid climate like Socotra, it would be impossible, during several months, to live in tents; and as the variations of the seasons compel the Bedowins to shift with their flocks in search of pasturage, it may be considered as a bountiful provision, that they are by these numerous excavations, with which the whole island abounds, provided with dwellings. All that is necessary to be done by the person who is about to occupy such a tenement, is with loose stones to portion off a certain space for himself and family, leaving the remainder to shelter his flocks.

I had reached one of these singular dwellings, and was about to enter, but before I could do so the natives fled in every direction, and I had consequently no opportunity of gratifying my curiosity on this occasion.

On January the 16th, not without some regret, we quitted our encampment, to proceed more towards the interior. It is useless geting vexed or displaying any irritation with Arabs, and I was in no degree surprised to find the impediments they constantly threw in the way of our further progress. Patience, (and we were not pressed for time) was our only remedy.

We only got away from this station by a forcible representation from the commander to the people at Tamarida. Then Hamed and the guide, who before had been unceasing in opposition, and had quitted us, again made their appearance, and we found roads, before stated to be impassable, now quite practicable, and tracts abounding in water, which he and his companions had before described as wholly destitute. They evince no shame on such occasions; with them a lie brings no discredit.

We had at first directed our steps towards a range of hills about seven hundred feet in height. The intermediate plain increases in width as we emerge from the pass. It is covered with dwarfish bushes, which grow in some places with a regularity that gives them the appearance of being planted rather by the hand of man than the caprice of nature. Their height is just sufficient to occasion considerable obstruction to the progress of our camels, and our bedding, which was packed outside, suffered so much on these occasions, that it soon became literally torn to shreds. These bushes disappear near the sea shore, where the soil is of a reddish colour and argillaceous nature; the country there presents gentle undulations, rising into rounded hillocks; grass of a fine quality covers the surface, upon which several herds of cows and some fine sheep were feeding. Towards the approach of sunset, we halted on a narrow ridge, beneath a huge mass of rock.

Some shepherds, passing at the foot of the hill with their flocks, fled directly they saw our party approach; but several old women made a bold stand, and bitterly reproached our guides for bringing strangers to their island. A few trifling presents of clothes, needles, &c. had the effect of restoring them to good-humour, and they furnished us with a small sheep, and an abundance of milk.

In the evening, two intelligent youths, each about sixteen, joined us, and, at first with some little alarm; but they were prevailed on to be seated, and were soon very inquisitive as to the objects of our journey. I soothed their apprehensions as well as I could, by representing myself as searching for coal, and that we were desirous of keeping on the best terms with the inhabitants, and in earnest of which, I stated that we should pay ready money for whatever we received.

The astonishment of these young savages at all they saw was very great. A dark lanthorn, a watch, the several astronomical instruments, especially, excited their surprise and astonishment, but nothing could induce them to touch either. They remained talking with us until a late hour, and then left, with a few other presents, in much good-humour.

The night was stormy, and it was well we took the precaution of securing our tent before we went to sleep, for the wind rushed through the vallies with so much violence that I expected every moment we should be blown over the hill.

Towards the morning we had several heavy showers, and our tent became completely saturated, so that between wind and rain, we obtained but little sleep, and were not sorry when morning dawned.

January 17th. After breakfast, we visited our friends of last night, who now testified no alarm at our appearance; they were seated under the shade of a *nebek* tree, and invited us to be seated on skins alongside of them. Our conversation with these people was maintained, through one of their number, in Arabic, few words only of this language being understood by the remainder of the party. It is evident from this that but little intercourse is carried on between the natives of the continent and those of the island.

What would our Sheffield manufacturers say

to the process of making a knife which we now witnessed. They had procured a portion of iron hoop from some whaler; this, when cut to the required length, was merely rounded at the extremity, and beat thinner on either edge; the lower end was fitted into a haft of hard wood, and the operation was then judged to be concluded; deep indentures were nevertheless visible in those which were handed to me as being finished; these, however, they said were to be removed by constant use.

Others of the party were also busily employed tanning skins, to serve for carrying either water, milk, or ghee. They use the outer bark of a species of acacia, called *taleo*, for this purpose, first immersing them in a solution, and afterwards rubbing the bark in its dry state over the skins. Adjoining to these mechanics several females were seated, in a natural bower, formed by the dense foliage of the tree I have noticed as resembling the weeping ash. Female curiosity seems as strong here as in more civilized parts of the world; and it was amusing on this occasion to observe their movements in order to gratify it. When admission was at first denied them by the men, they contrived, with coffee and under various other pretences, to approach, until further opposition was useless, and they had effected their object by seating themselves amidst the group.

Here I received intelligence that some inscriptions were to be found near to the sea-coast, and shortly after noon we set out to visit them. Journeying first to Cadhoop, we there filled our water-skins. Little wind was stirring, and the heat in those spots where it did not reach us was very great.

Two miles from Cadhoop we passed a shallow valley filled with date trees, which bears the name of Moree, and extends to a cape bearing the same name. In the winter season a powerful stream floods this; deep banks on either side prevent the water from running over and injuring the trees. Quitting the grove, our road skirted the sea-shore, where there were several fragments of red coral, madrepores, and a great variety of shells; I noticed a broad belt of white coral, extending for several yards into the sea; but neither that nor the shelly limestone with which it is so often mixed, occur so frequently as in the Red Sea, where it frequently rises up into hills, and extends in some places for several miles along the shores.

Quitting Ras Moree to the right, the bushes disappear, sandy tracts follow each other, and a ride of two hours brought us to the inscriptions we sought. They are cut on the face of a limestone-rock on the same level as the plains, and the portion over which they are found, irregularly strewn, measures three hundred paces in circumference; they strikingly resemble those found on the sea-coast of Western Arabia, and are, perhaps, rude representations of early Ethiopic. Besides these inscriptions, there are figures of men, of camels, &c., but more generally their feet are so cut in pairs, as if a soft rock had yielded to their weight. Crosses occur very frequently, as do also figures having a snake's head. Some religious edifice most probably was erected near this, of which there are, however, now no remains; a few rude huts are seen to the south-east.

In the evening we returned by a more southern route, skirting the roots of the seaward range of hills. We had now a clear bright sky, and the atmosphere was calm and still; the sun was sinking beneath the granite mountains, bathing their summits and wild peaks with its golden beams; a portion of the landscape still shared its brightness, but the sombre shadow of these masses throw their gigantic forms across the bosom of the vast ocean. I cast my eyes over its bright blue waters, now scarcely rippled by the breeze ; a steamer in the distance, breaking the uniformity of the horizon, was journeying to the Red Sea ; my thoughts followed her course to home and friends ; her decks were probably thronged with passengers, who while gazing on the island as they rapidly passed it, could form no idea that two of their countrymen were then watching with interest their course, and joyously anticipating a period when they too might be permitted again to visit their native land.

Our halting-place this evening was beneath some trees, and here we found a number of Arabs, who were preparing a marriage feast; two sheep, cut into small pieces, and boiled in an earthen pot, some rice, a few onions, and excellent dates, formed a meal, to which we were invited, and most gladly sat down. We did not attempt to conceal our mirth at the appearance of the two gallant candidates for nuptial bliss; they were both verging on seventy, and their wrinkled and decrepit appearance corresponded with their ages. They bore the numerous jokes of the party on the event with much equanimity. The eldest of the brides was said to be seventeen, and ten dollars was the sum demanded as a marriage portion.

Mahomed's permission to entertain a plurality of wives has been defended with some plausibility, on the ground that females decay in these climates far more rapidly than males—that, in plain English, a girl is married at thirteen, is a mother and in her prime at fifteen, and is faded at twenty-five.

After our meal and the customary ablutions, we repaired beneath another tree, where there was a portion of green sward. To my great surprise, I found a party had assembled for the purpose of dancing; an amusement, it would appear, by no means uncommon amidst the natives of the hills. Although the Arabs retain the same aversion to it as their brethren of the continent, a milder climate and the more invigorating atmosphere of these highland regions are conducive to this and other sports. Their present attempt was rude enough; one of their number chaunted a tune, while others joined in chorus; this was their only music, if such it might be termed. A number kept time, by a succession of jumps and bounds, while others stood in a circle, clapping their hands in unison to them.

Tobacco and a few presents added much to the innocent mirth of the party, and towards midnight the bridegrooms took their departure to join their fair partners, who with their parents were staying behind the neighbouring hills.

During the heavy showers which fell this night, our slaves were offered the interior of the tent: but they preferred remaining outside, lying on the ground, and wrapping themselves over with the thick mats which were used during the day to cover their camels. These slaves accompanied me during the whole of our tour, and more merry, more willing, or more faithful servants it would be impossible to obtain; nothing appeared to damp that good-humour with which they were always blessed, and in a cold or wet evening, similar to the present, a glass of spirits did not lessen either. It would have been, while thus journeying, ridiculous to have assumed, as far as our share of labour went, any superiority over the rest of the party, and whenever the occasion required it, both Mr. C. and myself joined without ceremony in every office, not excepting the preparation of our meals.

At first the Arab guides expressed astonishment that we who could command money should so do, but they soon became reconciled, and eventually it begot a confidence and cheerfulness that greatly heightened the pleasures of our tour.

I was very frequently (indeed whenever the weather permitted) compelled to sit up late, and make observations of the stars; and my companions would remain until they were concluded, watching with most intense interest every action; nothing would persuade them but that such operations had reference to astrological purposes. A cup of coffee and a pipe usually concluded the evening.

# CHAPTER V.

Noxious Insects—Storm—Singular Caverns—Devastation of Torrents—Nebek Trees—Reservoir of Rain Water—Singular Trees—Visited by the Mountaineers—their voracity—ascend the Mountains—deep and fertile Ravines—enter a Cave—Female astonishment—Presents—Invitation—Singular Habitations—Scene at Night—Physical appearance of Mountaineers—Golenseah—its indifferent Water—Quit Golenseah and again ascend the Mountains—Want of Water—Aloes—Civet Cats—Goats.

We continued our route, early on the following morning, along the base of the sea-ward range of mountains. Our track led over beds of torrents, or barren plains; pathway there was none. Along the banks of the former a few stunted bushes occur, mostly either the *nebek*, or a tree producing an acid fruit resembling the grape in its clustering appearance.

We breakfasted under the shade afforded by one of the latter; and, while thus seated, a female with a flock of sheep passed us, who immediately afterwards sent, unsolicited, a large bowl of milk. Two boys accompanying her had their mouths and nostrils covered with a small square piece of cloth, to protect, I was told, those parts from a noxious insect, to which the sheep are subject, and which, if they succeed in effecting a lodgment on the person, produce severe inflammation, and are extracted with difficulty.

Still following the bed of a stream, we crossed over huge fragments of limestone rock; a chain of pools extended on either hand, until we reached the termination of the valley. Here the country opens, and becomes more fertile and cheerful in its appearance. A plain, two miles and a half in width, was covered with grass, on which numerous flocks of sheep and goats were feeding. Crossing this, we again entered a mountainous track, and halted about sunset.

During the night the wind blew with great violence, and latterly it was accompanied with heavy rain. Our guides were very apprehensive of the forked lightning; and the thunder, as it rolled amidst the distant hills, was awfully grand: upon the whole, we were not displeased at the appearance of daylight, which enabled us to crawl out and warm our cramped limbs in the sun.

There were some caves in our neighbourhood, and to these we bent our steps. They were crowded with sheep and goats, and teeming with an almost incredible quantity of vermin. Two aged females were busily employed in weaving with a rude loom; others near, were making butter, by shaking the cream in skins; while a third party were constructing a net, which they use to entrap the wild goats of the mountains.

The surface of the interior of these caverns, some of which are of vast size, merely present to the eye of the spectator a succession of rounded masses blackened by smoke. Numerous small cells are occupied by pigeons and other wild birds, which remain there unmolested. Where the rock is exposed to the face of day, it receives in many places a tinge of red or blue, from thin and narrow veins containing particles of iron, which intersect it; and which not unfrequently contrast in a remarkable manner with the hue of clustering vegetation.

During the rainy season this part of the island is devastated by such powerful torrents, that our guides say the country cannot then be traversed, even on camels; and this the scattered appearance of many rounded masses of rock which line their course fully confirms. The bed of one of these streams measured three hundred yards in width; it was strewn with the trunks of trees which its waters had uptorn in their course. The nebek tree (*Lotus Nebca* of botanists) is very numerous here; its height usually averaging from twenty to thirty feet. The bark is light-coloured, rough, and crossed longitudinally by numerous fissures; the leaves are small and heart-shaped; the branches large, but foliage scanty.

Notwithstanding the hardness and length of the spines which grow intermingled with the leaves of this tree, camels, from the cartilaginous formation of their mouths, find no difficulty in feeding on it. The fruit in form and size resembles a cherry, and has a mild and pleasant, though peculiar flavour. The Arabs pound them in their rude mortars into paste, which they mix with *ghee*, and swallow with much apparent relish.

On the summit of a neighbouring hill I found an extensive reservoir of rain water, sufficiently capacious to supply the inhabitants of a very extensive district. Numerous trees fringed its margin, amidst the branches of which wood-pigeons, and a great variety of birds, were fluttering. From this we obtained an extensive view. A broad valley or plain, crossed by the same interminable torrents, separates the mountain ridge which girds the northern and southern parts of the island. Trees and occasional patches of verdure occur, but the general appearance is coarse and barren.

Here and in other parts we found two very remarkable trees, which I can find nowhere else described. They both grow in very rocky places, their roots seeking nourishment from the soil lodged in hollows. From the relative proportion between their height and diameter, and the few leaves, compared to the bulk of the trees, the most singular and grotesque appearances are often produced; their base not unfrequently covering a space more than equal to their height. The whole diameter of their trunk is so soft and spongy that it might with facility be divided with a common knife. A milky juice exudes from the leaves and branches of these trees, and is so exceedingly acrid, that if it reaches the eye the pain is nearly intolerable; yet camels and sheep feed with impunity on both.

There is also a tree here, the light and graceful form of which strikingly resembles that of the weeping ash of our own country. The leaves are easily agitated by the wind, and produce an appearance similar to those of the "light quivering aspen." We used to observe that a more beautiful or more tasteful mourner over a tomb could not perhaps be selected.

January 18th. Crossing the plain this morning in a south-east direction, we passed several Arabs, who cheerfully returned our salutation of peace; but the females generally fled: one, however, remained and testified her respect after the Arabian manner, by seating herself on the ground, with her back turned to the party.

We passed during our journey about half a dozen hamlets; some few solitary houses also appeared, scattered over the plain: a few bullocks, and occasionally a stray camel, mingled curiously in the scene.

Towards noon we halted in a narrow stony valley at the base of a range of mountains, so thickly wooded, that I found much difficulty in making my way up them. Occasionally I passed numerous flocks of sheep and goats; but the natives who were tending them exhibited so much alarm, that I could not venture to approach them. Springs of water are by no means frequently met with on the low land of Socotra; but I found a very copious one here, gushing in a clear full stream from the inner extremity of a cove. Numerous well-trodden paths denote how much this is frequented.

Shortly after our return to the tent, our guide succeeded in bringing there a party of the hill Bedowins, who had for some time been perceived in its vicinity, watching our operations. Their leader was a tall young man about thirty. He was invited within, while others seated themselves at the door of the tent. Astonishment at all they saw kept them mute for some time; they then proceeded with hurried curiosity to examine whatever presented itself to their notice. It was impossible to convince them that the motions of a watch were not those of a living animal.

A meal of rice and ghee, prepared by the slaves, had been in the mean time produced, and little solicitation was necessary to induce them to partake of it. The keenness of the mountain air, which these highlanders enjoy, sharpens their appetites to an extraordinary degree. Indians will astonish the European by the pile of rice which they will consume; and Arabs are not the abstemious people usually supposed; but both sink to insignificance compared with what this people will accomplish. I have observed them make four meals of animal food in the twenty-four hours, and yet partake of rice between whiles. Our three guides would finish the whole of a sheep, including the head and entrails, in this time; and our, comparatively-speaking, meagre fare excited the utmost surprise. "That a meal!" observed an Arab, when our breakfast on one occasion was placed before us; "why my youngest child (a boy eight years of age) finishes at each repast twice that quantity."

They conversed with us very freely on every subject connected with their customs and mode of life, not excepting their women, in whose praise they were very lavish. As the evening advanced, and tobacco and coffee had increased their good-humour, they readily acceded to my request for permission to roam over their hills; which pleased me the more, as our own guide, Hamed, had refused to escort us further, and I was unwilling, little as I at the time knew of the people, to trust myself, in his absence, without urgent necessity, wholly in their power.

One of the slaves, in the morning, remained with the tent, while the rest of the party set out for the mountains. An hour's creeping rather than walking, (for the bushes, under which lay the path, prevented us from standing upright,) brought us to the summit of the ridge. The vegetation, excepting a few dwarfish trees, now disappears; the rock, bleached by rain, and gales which continually sweep over the island, exposes its bleak and wasted aspect in every direction; its surface worn either into cells and cavities, or having narrow ridges between them. So sharp-pointed and rugged were the latter, that we found it painful, even with our shoes, to traverse them. Our staggering gait in such places afforded abundant amusement to our guides, who, accustomed to such paths from their earliest youth, tripped steadily over them.

From below, the unbroken appearance of the ridge had not prepared us to find that the country consisted of a pile of mountains, partially divided by deep glens and ravines; both possess a fine soil, and nourish a luxuriant vegetation.

We met with a large tree here, called by the natives *ukshare,* bearing fruit, which the natives find too acid for use, but designate it the wild grape; another tree, styled *bohain,* has a broad leaf resembling the English sycamore, which in size it rivals. The branches of these and other trees are interwoven in the most tortuous forms. We also passed several stately tamarind and fig trees. From the fruit of the former the natives distil a cooling and refreshing beverage; and the foliage of the latter affords at all times a grateful shade.

Crossing several of these ravines, and descending one of greater depth than the remainder, we found ourselves unexpectedly at the entrance of a huge cavern, tenanted at the moment only by women and children. The latter cast but one glance at us, and then ran screaming away. The females, as usual, stood their ground better, but continued uttering the monosyllable "Ha! ha!" to express surprise and astonishment.

Our new guides, after enjoying the scene for some time, condescended to explain who we were, and bowls of milk were then brought to us. The younger females of the party were remarkably fair and pretty; they did not wear veils, and made no attempt to conceal their faces. Their ears were decorated with a profusion of silver rings, and their necks with a string of dollars. We added a few trifling articles to this finery, the most considerable and esteemed of which were the buttons from Mr. Cruttenden's jacket. He had in an evil moment presented one to a fair damsel, and, to be equally complaisant to others, he found it necessary to completely strip his jacket.

The party now offered no objection to our taking up our quarters with them in the cave, which was upwards of one hundred and twenty paces in length. The entrance was nearly blocked up by a huge mass of rock, which, however, serves the double purpose of excluding the rain as well as the sun's rays. Circular stone walls with low narrow doors divided the interior into different apartments, each of which served a separate family, and the whole number of tenants was about forty. We purchased two sheep for the party, and leaving them to discuss these, I journeyed to the seaward face of the cliff, passing on my way there several other hamlets. I was accosted from one of these, with the query if I had come to seek a wife? a custom practised by the Arabs, who journey here, and effect this purpose by the payment of eight or ten dollars, unless the bride be particularly useful or handsome, when a much larger sum is demanded.

These huts were constructed of loose stones, and thatched with the dried branches of the date palm; an enclosure for sheep usually adjoins them.

We now followed a rocky path along the brink of a ravine, until we arrived at the extremity of the mountain ranges, which faces the sea, and terminates in an abrupt perpendicular precipice, about eight hundred feet in height. We descended a few yards, to a stairs-like projection, about two feet in width, serving as a terrace to a number of caves ranged by nature, like cells in a continuous line. Most of these were inhabited. A narrow wall prevents the cattle and children from falling over the precipice. But what frightful habitations these must be in the south-west monsoon, which blows directly on this part of the shore.

The hills on the opposite side of the island are, I have noticed, mostly clothed with vegetation; but the mural precipice, upon which I now stand, extending from one extremity to the other, has the same time-worn and grey appearance. The haziness of the weather prevented my making any observation on the island, and intermediate sea, between this and the African coast, of which so little is known; and I accordingly returned to the cave. I found Mr. C. quite domesticated with the party, all of which were preparing to discuss the sheep.

Before we had completed our evening meal it was quite dark, and, as the atmosphere of these regions was keen and cold, we found a fire quite necessary. There was no want of fuel, and a cheerful flame soon blazed before us; several others were lighted in different parts of the cave by the females, who, as in other parts of the East, eat their meals apart from the other sex. This custom, which is, as we perceive by the Bible, of the remotest antiquity, has doubtlessly arisen from a disinclination to see the two sexes grouped together in public; which, where hospitality is so freely dispensed, would otherwise be the case at nearly every meal. They carry the same principle even into the exercise of their public worship, where, if the females make their appearance at the same time as the men, they remain together in some portion of the spot to which the latter never approach.

We soon joined one of these circles, and were quickly addressed by a host of questions respecting the domestic life and manners of our countrymen; several of these were very shrewdly put, and, considering the great difficulty of making a simple people understand matters so wholly different from their own, their comprehension was equally acute.

The fame of our Indian rule would appear to have reached even this remote spot; for the natives spoke of its being probable that the Sultan of Kissen would dispose of the island to the English, without expressing any surprise, or betraying any aversion to such a change of masters.

"Whenever this takes place," observed an old man, "we shall at least have a government; at present we have none."

I answered by repeating the fable of the frogs who petitioned for a king, and then exchanged their hog monarch for one of more activity and energy. This afforded much amusement.

It was midnight before the party broke up; we then, at the suggestion of the Bedowins, collected some grass, upon which we spread our boat-cloaks, and were soon asleep. But it was destined our slumbers should not be unbroken. It rained violently, and sheep hastened for shelter from every direction to our cave. Their bleating alone would have been perhaps sufficient to have kept us awake; but, attracted by the grass on which we were lying, here again the sheep and goats continued to scamper and fight over us during the greater part of the night. Not so the natives, who, wrapped in skins, and stretched out on rocky ledges above the reach of our tormentors, continued uninterruptedly to enjoy their slumbers.

We passed the next two days in roving over this part of the island, and met every where with the same hospitable reception. The physical appearance of the mountaineers is highly favourable. The men are usually tall, with strong muscular well-formed limbs; a facial angle as open as that of Europeans; the nose slightly acquiline; the eyes lively and expressive; the teeth good, and the mouth well formed. Their hair is worn long, and curls naturally, but, unlike that of the natives of Madagascar, or Africa, without approach to a woolly or crisp texture: beards and whiskers are generally worn, but moustaches very seldom.

This singular people have few characteristics in common with the Sumaulis, differing, indeed, in many respects essentially from either that people or any other class of Africans which I have seen. Their complexion varies very much, some being as fair as the inhabitants of Surat, while others are as dark as the Hindus on the banks of the Ganges. Although they walk over the worst ground with an erect gait, and bound over the rocks like antelopes, yet from constantly traversing their mountains, they have contracted a habit of turning in their toes, which while crossing the plains, gives a slight defect to their gait; but, independent of this, the generality were models of strength and symmetry.

They display a little foppery in their mode of dressing the hair: some frizzle it in a manner similar to that of the Beshari Arabs on the coast of Egypt; others allow it to flow in natural ringlets; but the greater number braid it into plaits, and then confine it with a cord of their own hair. Their skins are clear and shining, remarkably free from any cutaneous disorders: many are, however, scarred, from the application of hot irons; a mode of cure for local complaints here, in as great repute as with the Arabs.

We find amidst the females the same symmetry of form, the same liveliness of expression; but their complexion does not vary in an equal degree, few being darker than the fairest of the men, and when young, they are rarely otherwise than pretty. The legs of such as are advanced in age are, especially amongst those who reside on the low land, of an astonishing thickness. Their dress is simple enough; a wrapper, made from goat's hair, girds their waist, and a loose cloth is thrown over their shoulders. Necklaces, made of red coral-coloured glass, or amber, are much worn, together with the earrings which I have before noticed. They always go unveiled, although on some occasions they are rigidly excluded from the society of the other sex.

We afterwards returned to our tent, and on the following day resumed our journey, by the same valley as that by which we had arrived, until we reached its termination, when we struck off to the westward for a village named in the map Golenseah. The country, barren at first, improved as we advanced, and we halted about sunset amidst an exuberant vegetation. Some of the natives joined our party here; one of whom was shown his cave on a hill, through a telescope. The instant he caught a glimpse, "It is the work of the devil!" said he, throwing the glass on the ground, and making off with all possible celerity.

We obtained but little sleep, in consequence of an abundance of flies, musquitoes, and other tormenting insects. Even our slaves complained.

Happy to quit our new abode, an hour's riding brought us to the foot of a pass; hence we followed a small stream, which supplies Golenseah with water; and about noon reached that village, off which I found the *Palinurus* lying. This village, or rather hamlet, contains a few wretched houses and huts, occupied by about fifty families, who gain a subsistence by fishing; their boats serving also to supply whalers and other vessels which occasionally touch here for water. Some pools in the vicinity of the houses furnish this, but its quality is very indifferent. Iron tanks on ship-board have the almost invaluable property of precipitating noxious matters, and thereby greatly purifying water; but we did not find, after some weeks, the unpleasant taste or smell removed from that which we obtained here.

Thames water ranks very high with seamen, but that in casks requires some months to purify itself. In iron tanks this is not the case; the water after a few days is brought up quite clear. Before this invention, which has so materially contributed to the health of our seamen, I look back with horror to the loathsome draughts I have been compelled to swallow, in the hot weather of the Persian Gulf. It will be unnecessary to say more than that the lids of the wooden tanks in which it was contained were but too frequently left off, and rats, cockroaches, &c. found their way into, but could not escape from them.

With the exception of a few wretched sheep, no other supplies can be obtained here, and the natives are bigotted and silly. Its harbour renders this station of some importance, because it affords excellent shelter during the north-east monsoon, and if a coal depôt were required at this season, none on the island could be found better adapted.

Having again bid my companions on board farewell, on January the 24th I journeyed to the shore, with an intention of completing my tour.

At some future day, should any English

traveller at Golenseah preserve a recollection that one of his countrymen had wandered over the island, let him from the anchorage cast his eyes to the mountainous wall, which forms its western extremity, and rises almost perpendicularly to the height of two thousand feet; then ask himself if it be possible for a human being, far less for a beast of burthen, to scale it. He would doubtless do as I did, when the proposal was first made by the natives, treat it with ridicule.

Our guides removed every thing from the backs of their camels, which was carried up by the villagers during the night; and, on the following morning, we commenced the ascent. The face of the cliffs presented a succession of ledges resembling gigantic stairs; and along these led the road, often not more than a foot in width, and frequently approaching the edge of a precipice of vast depth. In some places the rock was even so smooth that we deemed it needful to take off our shoes; yet there followed our camels close behind, puffing from the great steepness of the ascent, but still making their way with comparative ease and security.

A dark rich soil on the ledges nourishes a variety of trees, and numbers of aromatic plants shed a grateful perfume, and I made some valuable additions to my botanical collection. During the night a copious dew had fallen, every tree or bush teemed with moisture, and we received from each, as we grasped their trunks to aid our progress, not that mute salutation which endears the mimosa to the solitary traveller on the desert, but one in the cool of the morning less agreeable—a complete shower bath; before we reached the summit we were completely drenched.

Here we were amply repaid, both in change of climate and the appearance of the country. Fahrenheit's thermometer, which indicated 86° below, now rose to about 69°. From the altitude we had attained, every thing was spread out in beautiful detail at our feet. The day was serene and bright; a meridian sun lighted up all around with splendour. Below, a fresh breeze was sweeping along, driving far to seaward the morning mist: yet the vast expanse of ocean, with its horizon elevated to nearly the same apparent level as ourselves, was silent and tranquil, its surface, with the exception of a silvery line of surge which rippled and glistened along the white beach, being wholly unruffled; while many and beautiful hues were reflected from its party-coloured coral, sandy or rocky bottom,—blending themselves into a lively green—thence to the purple of ocean—and again fading away in the distance to a vapour-like blue, which rendered it difficult to distinguish sea from sky. The white canvas of our boats, then pushing off from the ship, and our native vessel also beating into the bay,—the village of Golenseah, its palm trees and lakes of fresh water,—all added to, or heightened the picture.

I was so pleased with the neighbourhood that I remained here several days, making excursions to various parts of the island. We found a never-failing source of amusement in these wanderings. Every thing was new. The country, its productions, and inhabitants, afforded abundant and constant food for observation. In the evening we returned to enjoy our dinner by a cheerful fire.

Although so elevated, this part of the island has neither wells nor running streams; and as the natives are not far enough advanced in civilization to sink tanks, they depend for their supply on the water which is left in hollows by the rain. At present there was an abundance of fine grass, but they care not for making hay; and the great part is trodden under foot, and destroyed by the cattle while feeding on it.

Each of the cottages which are found amidst

these mountains has attached to it a small enclosure, in which millet is grown. The process is simple enough: the loose stones are removed from the surface, and with them a wall is built to keep off the cattle; the ground is loosened with a pointed stick, and formed into small squares, the grain sown, and the operation judged to be complete. This millet will keep uninjured for a long time, and when their supply of dates and milk fails them, it forms a staple article of their food. They merely bruise it between two stones, mix it with water, and make it into cakes. We made several attempts to eat these, but they are so rough and coarse that we could never reconcile ourselves to them.

At first the natives exhibited some shyness towards us, but at length they became more reconciled, and subsequently crowded round the tent in great numbers, each bringing a small offering of dates, milk and butter; for which we gave them scissors, thread, &c. Dollars appeared in small request, but the men eagerly sought after our clasp knives and tobacco boxes. When they heard that we were provided with medicines, they were unceasing in their applications for relief; the men complaining principally of what would be concealed in Europe, and the females of sterility. But, judging from numerous groups of children, neither appeared to prevail to any alarming extent.

The sextant with which I had been taking some observation, to my great dread, underwent a minute examination, but they could make nothing of it. It was an inverting telescope which excited the most intense surprise. I made one of the servants stand at a short distance from the tent, while they looked at him through it. Not one of them could be brought to occupy his place, and the females ran screaming away as soon as I proposed it to them.

It being the period of the Ramadan, they left us at sunset; but a great number of females, the most noisy and talkative of our former visitors, returned in the evening. Numerous and almost incessant were their questions. Had we any sheep, goats, or bullocks in our country? Did we ever pray? What number of wives had the English sultan? Were we married? But beyond all, and in this the men joined them, what were we doing here, writing down, as they had seen us, hills, trees, and flowers? They could not comprehend that we had any other motive than eventually to take possession of the island. They laughed at, as too absurd, the idea that so much trouble and expense should be incurred in measuring the island, or in ascertaining in what respect its productions differed from those of other parts of the world.

The aloe, they remarked, had especially engaged our attention. This plant has rendered Socotra famous from the earliest period. It is found growing on the sides and summits of the limestone mountains, at an elevation of from five hundred to three thousand feet above the level of the plains. The plant appears to thrive only in parched and barren places; its leaves are plucked at any period, and, after being placed in a skin, the juice is suffered to exude from them. This is afterwards carried principally to Muscat, where the price varies according to the quality, from two to four shillings the English pound. Socotran aloes, if care were taken in collecting them, would be the finest in the world; but this is not the case, and their value becomes proportionately deteriorated.

When the authority of the sultans of Kisseen was better acknowledged than at present, they monopolized the whole produce of the island; and stone walls, dividing its surface into separate portions, were carried with immense labour over hill and dale. These still remain, but now any one collects the plant, when or where he thinks proper; and this they only care to do when the arrival of a ship or buggalow creates a demand. Every part of the island affords this useful plant, but more especially the western, where the surface is thickly covered for miles. In 1833, only two tons were exported.

When we left, the whole of the party assembled to bid us farewell, and we received much assistance from them, in packing our camels, and other kind offices. The following day we reached a small building, which our guides described as having formerly served as a place of worship. It was a rude tenement, constructed of loose stones, eighteen feet long and fifteen feet broad, and surrounded by a rude wall. I saw neither inscriptions nor crosses; but there was a stone within, which appeared as if it had been covered with red paint, and there is reason also, from other causes, to believe, that before the introduction of Mahomedanism, a species of litholatry was practised in Socotra.

Some discussions have taken place with respect to the religion followed by the earlier inhabitants of this island. At the period of Sir Frederick Roe's visit he found Nestorian Christians. To avoid the persecutions of this sect in Asia, there is little doubt but that numbers of that persuasion fled here; at present, every individual in Socotra professes himself to be a Mahomedan.

In the evening we heard the cry of several civet cats close to our tent: these, as far as I know, are the only wild animal found here. They were frequently brought in for sale, and are very numerous. One I purchased, and carried with me to Bombay; but there, from the damp weather, it died. It was a female, measuring, including the tail, two feet nine inches. Its hair was long and not very fine, its colour dark grey streaked with vertical bars of black; the head small and handsome, resembling, in that and its general form, the mangousta. It was always fed on rats, which it seized from the trap in which they were caught, and killed instantly. The fore legs were short and black, with five separate and strong toes on each foot; the hinder were much longer; and while seizing its prey, the tail assisted in turning and leaping; with this I have seen it strike the ground so forcibly as to cause the end to bleed. Its temper in general was good, but if provoked exhibited much ferocity.

It is remarkable that neither hyenas, jackals, monkeys, nor other animals common to the shores of either continent, are found here; not even the antelope, which is very numerous on many other islands off the coast of Arabia.

It will be seen by the preceding part of this narrative, that goats and sheep are found in every part of the island. The former are small and lean, with slender legs, and are of indifferent flavour. They have not the ponderous tail of those of Africa and Arabia. Their carcasses, when divested of offal, frequently weighed no more than ten pounds; and our seamen in jest remarked, that they would then answer admirably as lanterns. The Bedowins, to prevent their getting the rot, wash them every three months. Their wool is used for making the thick cloaks so generally used in Arabia.

Goats are so numerous that the inhabitants keep no account of them. There are three kinds: the milch goat, of which much care is taken; another, of a reddish colour, with long shaggy hair, apparently common property; a third, the wild goat, a noble-looking animal. It is found amidst the loftiest portions of the mountains, and frequently in the most lonely glens. As its flesh is much prized by the Bedowins, they are at some pains to catch it. This they effect by spreading a net across its tracks, and, making their appearance above, the frightened animal darts down, and is caught in the toils.

## CHAPTER VI.

Discharge our Guide—Furious Storm—Rough treatment of a Camel—Beauty of the Scenery of Socotra—Fears of the Inhabitants—Date Groves—Attempt to reach the Summit of the Mountains—Unexpected Opposition—Quarrel—Sunday—Feast of the Ramadan—Quit the Town—Itinerant Merchant—Female Curiosity—Abundance of Water—Mode of milking Goats—Visit the Granite Mountains.

One of our guides (Hamed) continued to give us so much trouble that I was compelled to discharge him. Everywhere I found that he was tampering with the natives, either to defraud us, or, by misrepresentation, to create unfavourable opinions as to the object of our tour. One great feature which conduces to successful travelling in the East, is to allow yourself to be cheated with your eyes open; but let this be done by the people of the country, not your own servants, and if disputes arise between the two, the traveller will do well if he incline more to favour the former than the latter. Relying on the forbearance we had hitherto manifested, or perhaps enamoured of his good fare, Hamed was contumacious, and intimated his intention of remaining, whether it pleased me or not. "We shall see," observed I, "in the morning; if then I find you here I will break your bones." He did not compel me to perform my promise, but decamped during the night.

The day was warm and sultry, passing clouds swept over the sky until noon, when we had heavy showers, and stormy gusts of wind. The fury of these blasts was almost inconceivable; pent up by the hills on either hand, they roared through the valleys with a strength which threatened to carry all before them; even our camels were occasionally compelled to turn or lie down. Branches of trees, sand, pebbles, and even birds, were swept along by the current. Water was hurled past in sheets, and we heard from the Bedowins that their cattle, by similar storms, were frequently driven over the precipices.

Sunset brought us fair weather. Our guides represented the inhabitants at the spot where we halted to be less honest than in other parts of the island. As far as robbery went, we had little cause, however, for apprehension, because our instruments were all of value with us, and of these I knew they entertained too much dread even to handle them. A few minutes after we had halted twenty or thirty collected amidst the hills, and approached us in a body.

Seating themselves beside the tent, they conversed for some time, when one of their number inquired if I had the means of preventing them from taking possession of what was with me ? A tree, at the distance of ten or twelve yards, was before us. " Nothing more than this," observed I, levelling a double-barrelled rifle pistol at the trunk, and, by a lucky chance, sending both balls through it. Away scampered the whole party; they probed the orifices with their fingers, looked at each other in mute astonishment, and then quietly slunk away. My pistols having detonating locks, they were ignorant of the manner in which the powder had been ignited, and the suddenness of the act did not lessen their terror. I was no more troubled with similar questions.

Here there was a very capacious reservoir of water, the sides and bottom of which were lined with stone, but the natives had neglected to roof it over,—which, to prevent the waste by evaporation, is always done in Arabia and Persia. There they select some spot to which, as in this case, water-courses naturally lead; then they sink a tank. Baked by the intensity of the sun's rays, the surface of the soil, hard as a tile, does not permit the water to leak through, but whenever rain falls it runs so rapidly off that a single shower frequently fills such reservoirs.

Did the inhabitants of Socotra avail themselves of this method, they would not, as they do now, suffer so frequently from drought.

Matter had formed in the foot of one of our camels, and my guides effected its discharge in a cruel but very simple manner; securing its legs and mouth by strong cords, they turned the animal, roaring and struggling, on its side; then thrusting a red hot iron to the depth of several inches into the part affected, they finished the operation by scarring the foot with several transverse bands. I advocated at least a halt, to complete the cure. "Quite unnecessary," said his master, as the animal limped past; "he will go better when he warms." In the East the brute species are rarely treated with cruelty, especially camels, which, enjoying as they do the credit of being the most patient, are nevertheless the most troublesome to manage of perhaps any domestic animal.

In Arabia, whenever a caravan halts, the legs of the camels are tied, and they are not permitted to rise from the encampment; here, however, they were permited to stray whither they pleased, and, with one leg fastened, were frequently found in the morning high up amidst the mountains. Here the leaves of trees form their principal food; one meal of beans only being daily supplied to them. The Socotrian camel is large, and is capable of carrying a very heavy burthen. I believe they were originally brought from the Arabian coast.

It was very amusing to observe the terror of the females we passed on our several journeys here; no sooner did they catch a glimpse of our party than, screaming out "Weelah, weelah!" off they ran, carrying their children either on their backs or beneath their arms. One damsel finding that her progress was impeded by her lower habiliments, threw them without hesitation over her head; and another, similarly situated, dropped her only lower garment, and effected a swift escape without it. I could not but observe that their legs, compared to those of the men, were of an astonishing thickness, and Nature, in that part of the human frame which has with Hottentots attracted the attention of our physiologists, appears here to be not less bountiful.

We were now journeying in the direction of the granite mountains, which occupy nearly a central position on the island. The valley along which we passed was narrow and steep; hills, perpendicular as a wall, rose to a great height on either hand; huge boulders, over which, from their smoothness, our camels found their way with difficulty, are strewn along its bed; neither huts nor inhabitants are visible; and in the general aspect of the scenery I was strongly reminded of the wild and savage glens in the vicinity of Mount Sinai.

It has been my good fortune to have traversed much of the East, and to have witnessed every variety which has been there assumed by Nature. That of Socotra yields to none in wildness and romantic grandeur. Thus, in the evening we pitched our tent in the centre of an enormous hollow in the mountains, not less than three miles in diameter. At but a few yards distance a beautiful stream murmured its gentle course; not a breath of wind could reach us, and the wild and plaintive notes of the wood pigeon alone broke the silence and solitude of the scene. Grey, steep, and towering, the granite spires rose to an elevation of 5,000 feet, and the geologist would have derived great interest at witnessing fragments of the lower formation, either borne up between two peaks, or curiously wrapped like a mantle round others. The junction also between the limestone and granite was beautifully exposed to view; appearing as if a huge mass in a state of fusion had subsided over the lower, which in spires reared themselves beneath.

Not far from where we had encamped there was a small date grove, and although no one was left to take charge of the trees, yet we were told the fruit was never pilfered. For ages have this race of people remained free from the intrusion of strangers, and our brief sojourn created so much alarm that I was not sorry to leave; for we occupied their watering-place, and none would venture in consequence to visit it. Sunday, my Nubian servant, dressed as an European, unexpectedly confronted one of this people. Greater astonishment and terror could not have been exhibited had it been his Satanic majesty, for whom probably he was taken. Scrambling up the almost perpendicular precipice, the terrified Bedowin bounded from rock to rock, and was soon lost to view.

From this point I made an attempt to scale the mountains, but after ascending about 2,000 feet, our further progress was arrested by a precipice so steep as to leave us little chance of scaling it. From every direction narrow valleys led to the hollow beneath, and in the rainy season the collection of water there must be great. All the lower portion of these mountains was covered with bushes and trees. A solitary dragon's-blood tree sometimes may be observed on the summit of a peak, but otherwise the summits of the mountains are divested of vegetation. Here there was little to denote that man had trodden the dreary wilderness. My companions had strolled to some distance, and I was seated, making a sketch of the scene before me, when three or four Bedowins made their appearance. They had evidently been watching us for some time, and took advantage of my being alone, to approach. They were armed with thick clubs, and at first seemed inclined to quarrel; but I had collected a few words of their language, and contrived with these and other artifices to keep them amused until the return of my guides, who explained matters to them, and then a few presents sent them away in much good-humour.

We returned to Tamarida, taking up our old quarters at Abdallah's house. We now discovered that one of the Arab chiefs from the opposite coast had made his appearance in the island, and strictly forbidden any assistance being given to the furtherance of our tour. I had yet to visit the eastern portion of the island, and was anxious, if possible, to conciliate this personage; addressing therefore a letter to him, in which I recalled to his recollection the promise made by the old Sheikh Omar-bin-Tary of Kisseen, I hinted that, after permission to undertake the tour had been so unequivocally given by him, my government would not brook the interference of another party. While awaiting his answer, for he was then employed at Golenseah collecting the annual tribute, we were nearly getting into a serious scrape with the town Arabs, who, ever jealous of all our motions, assumed over the other inhabitants a far greater degree of importance; thus, they insisted upon the privilege of entering our apartments when and in any number they pleased.

"Such," said they, "is our custom."

"But such," replied I, "is not ours;" and we closed the doors.

We may submit "to do as Rome does" in savage countries, where to do otherwise is unavoidable, but this was not the case here, and the readers will conceive how annoying it is when you are employed reading, writing, or at meals, to have a dozen people watching and commenting on every action.

My non-conformity was received in high dudgeon, and one person named Ali, more contumacious than the others, and perhaps presuming upon our being alone, attempted to enter by force; upon which I directed my servant, Sunday, as soon as he entered the room to pitch him headlong out of it; which he did, with the same coolness as he would have done had he ejected a cat.

Sunday was a faithful and invaluable servant. His history is somewhat interesting. I was fond of leading him to discourse on himself, his country and his friends. He preserved a distinct recollection of his father's hut, and the various articles of furniture within it, and the kindness of an old village priest, who taught him the *koran*. They subsisted principally by hunting, and it was on one of these excursions, when about twelve years of age, that he was kidnapped by some of his own relations, and sold to a slave-dealer at Buber on the Nile. Thence he was driven across the desert twenty days, to Suakin, a port on the Red Sea. At this period it was, as I have before noticed, considered advisable to man the East-India Company's vessels of war with Africans, and he was accordingly nominated and received on board. His figure was tall and thin, but well proportioned; he had the crisp and curly head of the negro, without his flattened nose or thick lip; on the contrary, his features were regular and pleasing, partaking more of the Abyssinian than the negro cast.

By the wish of the sailors, like Robinson Crusoe's Man Friday, he received his soubriquet, John Sunday, from the day on which he came on board; and this, in their opinion, furnished an additional reason for which he should be speedily made a Christian. But this was not so easily to be done. He was as wild and active as a goat; for some days it was impossible to convince him, but that he was destined to be eaten; and he had an especial horror of the boatswain, who, to a most capacious mouth, added a truly formidable range of teeth; he had but to expand the one, and display the other in a grin, and off the poor little fellow would scamper, and take shelter in some obscure nook in the hold, from whence it was difficult, for some time, to dislodge him.

As he had accompanied the caravan the whole time on foot, his condition at first was very miserable; but for some time he refused food, under an impression that we were merely desirous of rendering him the better fattened for our epicurean palates. When he got rid of this dread, by perceiving that we persisted in eating in the same manner as other folks, he gradually acquired our habits, was taught to eat with a knife and fork, "like a Christian," as his now great friend the boatswain said; and at length, to the sailors' great delight, he was taught to take the half allowance of grog, which boys in a vessel of war are always permitted to draw. For some time, however, I was afraid that this gradual violation of the Temperance Society rules of his countrymen was a source of more gratification to the boatswain's friends than himself; for when he first took charge of Sunday, it was observed, by those malignant persons who are ever desirous of peering into the actions and affairs of others, that the notes of his pipe after meals, before he called all hands, were richer, more mellifluous, more lengthened, and terminated in a smarter flourish, than before; all of which however, it was thought, diminished in proportion to Sunday's increasing capacity for relieving his friend from the painful duty of swallowing the pernicious poison aforesaid.

Sunday manfully resisted pork for some months, nor did he ever take kindly to it; the noise it made in frying used to surprise and disgust him; if he could escape, he would never remain near it.

I am not surprised at this aversion, arising as much from religion, as from the unmitigated disgust which all must imbibe who have only seen the swine in the East. There it is a tall, gaunt, half-famished and wholly ferocious-looking brute, which performs the office of scavenger.

When Sunday had, in some measure, mastered our language, myself and brother officers amused ourselves with teaching him reading and writing. On most points his progress and comprehension were on a par with the mere European, excepting in the power of figures, which *on paper* he never could be made to understand; but set him to make a bargain, however complicated the details, and it very soon became apparent that his talents were not to be despised.

He attached himself at an early period to me, and has accompanied me on journeys for many hundred miles, in sickness, in health, in danger, or in privation; and I ever found him the same brave and faithful creature. I had but one fault to find with him: his desire to save me from being fleeced, frequently got him into scrapes with the natives. No reasoning with him could prevent this; which was a great annoyance to me, for the reason I have given a few pages back, relative to travelling in the East.

Sunday often spoke with much feeling of his mother, his sisters, and other relations he had left behind him; and I used to inquire if he was desirous of returning to them? He always despondingly replied, that if they had escaped the same fate as himself, which he learned that they had not, the difference in their religion would prevent them from ever receiving him. He once met a fellow villager in Egypt, but was so ashamed at having fallen from the faith of his fathers that he could not muster courage to speak to him, and enquire into the fate of those he still held dearest.

Those who have sought to degrade the African below the ordinary level of the human race, describe them as possessing the social affections in but a weak degree. My own experience enables me to give a decided negative to such an assertion, for in this respect I should place them far above the Asiatics.

On the following day, I had seated myself, and was reading in the upper part of the house, when my attention was arrested by the screaming of women, and I perceived several Arabs with drawn swords rushing towards an adjoining house. One of Abdallah's daughters seeing me lean over the parapet, screamed out, "Why they are murdering your servant!" Down I rushed, and hastening to the scene of action, there found Ali on the ground, and Sunday, with the ferocity of a tiger, fastened with both hands on his throat. Abdallah, our host, had reached the combatants before me, and was half frantic in his endeavours to prevent the Arabs from deciding the affair by cutting Sunday to pieces. Releasing his opponent from Sunday's grasp, I directed him to follow me. The Arabs were highly excited: they flourished their swords over our heads, spit at, and abused me, and could a leader have been found, all would soon have been over with the party.

When we entered the house, Sunday told me that he was quietly gathering vegetables in an adjoining garden, when the Arab came unawares behind him, and struck him with a thick club on the head; yet, thanks to his Nubian birth for the thickness of his skull, and his English education for the use of his fists, he retaliated with interest, and but for interference would doubtless have come off the victor.

The Cadi had been sent for, and he now arrived, and a deposition was taken before him. Ali's wounds were sworn to as alarming and serious, though in truth they were merely scratches, which he had deservedly received. When the deputation waited on me, representing that a Christian slave had smote a Mussulman, I thought matters had gone far enough.

"None," said I, "in the employ of the English are slaves, but servants, who, so long as they serve us with fidelity, we consider ourselves bound to protect with our lives, and any further attempt to molest Sunday I shall consider as addressed to myself."

The reader will smile at the high tone which I on this occasion assumed; but with a class similar to those amidst which I was then placed, it was as well to feign a superiority which I in reality did not possess. A sufficient degree of confidence in this assumption, provided it be tempered with judgment, is one of the best qualities which a traveller can possess. How strikingly we see this exhibited in Bruce's journey through the wild Galla and Abyssinian countries! How often do we not find him overcoming perils and difficulties, by the assumption of a carriage and demeanour implying a right (which the natives felt they dared not dispute) to direct the services of those who were with him—more, in fact, than any of their own chiefs would display. His vanity,—that failing which in Europe even his best friends never sought to shield him from,—became, on his travels, one of his best safeguards. His immense stature, his skill in martial exercises, his knowledge of languages, and his undaunted courage, all entitle Bruce to the appellation he will in after-years enjoy, of the "prince of travellers."

Ali, Sunday's discomfited foe, still hungered for revenge; and the strict watch kept on him by his friends (not out of any love to us, but fear of retaliation from the vessel,) alone prevented his making a second attack. We generally walked out together well armed, and keeping a good look-out, Ali had no chance but to make an open attack,—which was, however, not his object. Most anxious, therefore, became the inhabitants that we should proceed to our vessel, which we supposed was, in the prosecution of her survey, somewhere on the southern side of the island.

The 10th completed the full period of the Ramadan; but great was the grief of the most pious of my neighbours when the cloudy weather rendered it impossible to discern the moon, and they would not therefore consider the fast as concluded. Not so the greater number, who, less fastidious, set to work in good earnest, passing the night in all the customary feasting and rejoicing. Every matchlock or pistol the town could afford, was fired as long as their ammunition lasted; lanthorns, torches, and lamps illumined the houses; in the streets large bonfires were lighted, and some rude fire-works discharged until daylight; even the slaves obtained a holiday, singing, dancing, and smoking until they were half frantic. With us sleep was out of the question; so, following Haroun Al Raschid's example, we passed the night in wandering from party to party, in search of adventures; but we were neither regaled with any of those fascinating tales which it was his good luck to hear, nor to meet with much worth relating. It was thought, in a conversation of some continuance, that my countryman had worked a more favourable impression on the spouse of one of the merchants, than was considered, notwithstanding the general license, consistent with the husband's security of mind. Amidst themselves the freedom of speech and intercourse was however unbounded; women were grouped indiscriminately with the other sex, chattering and laughing without reserve.

Bedowins from the hills traversed the streets, receiving presents of rice from the town's folk, They either advanced in single line, dancing, singing, and flourishing their clubs, or they followed each other two abreast. But what pleased me more than any other part of these ceremonies, was to see, after all in the morning had been seated, perfumes burnt, and rose-water sprinkled over his guests, our venerable host, Abdallah, rise up, extend his arms in the direction of those assembled, and invoke on them, with much solemnity, the blessings of God and the Prophet. Some of the most zealous, I thought, cast their eyes towards us, half pitying infidels, who could not, or would not, thus worship their creator. The day passed off without the slightest interruption to the general harmony.

Sunday had been for some days suffering from an enlargement of the spleen, for which our old Bedowin female cupped him. First gently rubbing over the organ for about half an hour, she scarified the surface, placed a horn over the parts affected, and applying her mouth to an orifice in the upper part, by suction she exhausted the air, and then closed it with her thumb. This was repeated several times, until a sufficiency of blood was judged to have been withdrawn; and Sunday evidently received much benefit from this simple operation.

Tamarida is a wretched place to remain in,

being surrounded by swamps. We were troubled with swarms of flies during the day, and at night those industrious animals, whose labour it is so much more interesting to watch beneath a glass case than on our persons, would charge, while we lay down, in legions. Sleep was therefore out of the question, and we frequently remained, in consequence, smoking during the greater part of the night, in the court-yard. The coolness of the morning air would frequently rid us of these visiters, and then we esteemed it happiness could we but snatch an hour's brief slumber.

Wearied with our stay, we at length received an answer from the Arab chief; it was very laconic: "Let the Feringees," said he, "be closely confined to Tamarida until their vessel arrives." But Abdallah, avaricious and cunning, was not thus to be outwitted. Now that he was desirous of getting rid of us, the letter was kept a secret from all others, and a bargain was struck, in which, though it was to be represented to his neighbours that I was about to leave for the ship, the camels it was understood were hired by the month, and that I was to take them where I pleased. As a further blind, Mr. Cruttenden, whose acquaintance with the habits of the people made him at all times at home with them, remained behind as a hostage, as they were pleased to term him.

Again, with a light heart, on February 13th, I recommenced my tour. My journeys were so short that I shall not give a continuous diary, but convey the reader much faster over the ground than I could travel. My first object was to see and communicate with the ship; then to journey to the eastern extremity of the island. I had no reason, from report, to expect much in addition to the information which I had already obtained; still I felt that sort of wish which the reader will I hope appreciate, to leave as little of the island untrodden as possible.

Passing several date groves, and occasional mounds of ruins, we found the country well watered, exhibiting at times a border of fine turf, and again equally arid and barren. The hamlets we passed were inhabited by Arabs, not less mongrel and intolerant than those of Tamarida; and such an outrageous clamour did they raise whenever I produced my sketch-book, that I afterwards took all my notes by stealth. One day, however, an old female of the same class surprised me sketching the outline of a hill. She was about to raise a disturbance, when I represented that it was but to please my harem on my return; and this satisfied her.

I have never witnessed, in any part of the world, a stronger feeling of intolerance than amidst this people: of course I do not mean the Bedowins. Occasionally some of our party would fall sick; and the horror they expressed at the bare possibility of the party dying and being buried on the island, left me no room to doubt but that they would perform their promise of disinterring the corpse, and flinging it with every indignity into the sea.

I was occasionally much amused to witness the consequence these people assumed when we halted; not unfrequently desiring us to move from their neighbourhood. We always turned this into a source of merriment, laughing and taking no heed of them. Perhaps a party of Bedowins would shortly after arrive; with them we were soon on excellent terms; a few presents were given; and did our former visitors strive to gain our good-will, we had nothing to say, and they usually walked away muttering that which I neither wished to hear nor comprehend.

Hardly had we left the date groves which form the eastern boundary of the plain, when it set in to rain heavily; the camels slipped about whenever we reached a muddy soil, and two or three received some heavy falls. On the rocks the inequality of their surface rendered the footing more secure, and they fared better.

Towards evening the weather cleared up, and the sun shone out with all that fierceness which, in a tropical climate, is usually experienced after rain. In its rays we spread our clothes to dry, and in the mean time sought some pools shaded by impending rocks, in which we bathed. On the smooth surface of a level plateau adjoining to one of these pools I pitched my tent. Gently the stream, calm and clear, sped its way onward, to lose its tiny waters in the vast ocean—a mere drop; yet typical of the space in the universe shared by those who now were watching its course. Aloft, on her silvery way, high soared the moon; there was not a breath of wind to agitate either the leaves of the trees or "sough over the water. I was fast yielding to the delicious softness of the scene, when—"Salam alicum,"* uttered in a clear confident voice, roused me.

"Alicum salam,"† returned I. "Be seated, friend."

"A thousand thanks. I have heard of you,"

* Peace be with you. † With you be peace.

observed my guest, "and curiosity brought me here to see you."

"Your name, O stranger?" inquired I.

"Abdallah."

"Most welcome, Abdallah."

Coffee was brought. I longed for a pipe; a cigar was offered; my guest had never seen and did not understand it, but a whiff of tobacco at any cost he must have. Stripping, therefore, the bark entire off a small branch of a tree, he, in a manner similar to what we should do when cutting a quill to make a pen, trimmed the end, and inserted therein a small perforated piece of wood; upon that was laid the tobacco, the fumes of which he inhaled.

I gained much information from this man, who left me a little after midnight to pursue his journey. He was one of those itinerant traders who traverse the island, collecting its produce from the natives. Hardy, good-humoured, and, for their class of life, even intelligent, their intercourse with strangers is more frequent than with others. Seldom have I met them but in merry mood, singing to the utmost extent of their voices; or, if not mounted on their camels, marching sturdily along. Every where is their appearance hailed with satisfaction. A Bedowin, when one of this class approaches, kills a goat, and feasts him as if a near and dear relative had returned. Even their bargains are conducted in equal good faith and good humour.

Ascending the valley in the morning, at the gorge of which we had passed the night, about mid-day we were sheltering ourselves from the heat of the sun, when a merry group of damsels, taking advantage of the absence of their lords, quitted their spinnets and churning of butter, and boldly resolved to hold a converse with white people. Onward they came, determined to make the most of their time. My clothes, spread out in the sun to dry, first attracted their attention. How minutely they examined them—how joyous was their mirth as they were told or discovered the purposes to which each article was to be applied. So much delight was exhibited by one damsel, who, in imitation of what she saw on me, slipped on a pair of white pantaloons, and so excessive was her admiration when she had accomplished this feat, that I could not do otherwise than beg her acceptance of them. To another I was then obliged to be equally liberal. As the pair, proud of their new habiliments, strutted to and fro before me, to the delight of themselves and companions, it was impossible to resist joining in the general merriment. The pockets puzzled them not a little; but by placing pins, needles, thread, &c. within them, I very soon explained their use. Perhaps in England my new acquaintances would not be considered handsome; yet there was an expression of much shrewdness and good-humour in their countenances and dark bright eyes.

"Twenty-six years of age," said one of them to me, "and not yet married? Why who takes care of your house, and prepares your meals?"

Briefly as their voluble inquiries would admit, did I endeavour to palliate the condition of a bachelor so far advanced in years; but vain was the attempt; nothing in their opinion could compensate for so many years absence from connubial bliss. Much commended, however, was our practice of adhering to one wife.

Fears of the return of their husbands curtailed the stay of my most interesting visitors, so they took their leave. I offered my hand; they laughed, but extended theirs when I assured them that such was our English custom.

"We must go now," whispered one who lingered the longest; "because if our husbands find us here, they would beat us; but remain till the morrow, and then," added she, "when they have gone out with their cattle, we will stay with you all day; and listen to tales about your wonderful country."

I was sorry to be obliged to refuse. No one inquired during their stay if I was a Mahomedan; usually the first question asked by all classes.

From this spot we followed a rapid stream, which occasionally took a sweep round the mountain, at the base of which it glided in clear full course. Hills, to the height of 500 to 1,000 feet, rose on either hand, mostly of feldspar or porphyry. We were continually compelled to cross this stream, which delayed us much; and our guides were apprehensive for the feet of their camels; ulcers, when they are kept on damp or marshy places, form there, which are difficult and tedious to cure. Copious night dews wetting the grass will produce the same effect. Thus, in India, where the rains are violent, the camel is rarely found to thrive. In general, camels are averse to taking the water; yet when tormented by flies and other insects, they may be perceived hastening to a brook or pool, in which they immerse themselves.

At length we emerged from the mountains, and entered a low sandy plain, called by the Arabs Noged. Its width averages about three miles, and it extends nearly the whole length of the southern side of the island. On the coast there is a continuous line of sand-hills, which have been driven up by the force of the south-west monsoon, which sweeps along here with all the fury of a tempest. Similar in its general features to Arabia, we meet on this plain many of the shrubs and aromatic plants common to hot countries. The rak, with its roots embedded in sand, and its fragrance perceptible from a great distance, and its lovely green foliage, offers a curious contrast to the glistening white sand. The water on this plain is brackish, and we could not tolerate it.

No ship was in sight, and as we halted, an old man, perceiving we were strangers, approached and pressed our occupying his house, out of which he assured us he had just turned his wives. Declining his offer with many thanks, we pitched our tent. Small as it was, this appeared so superior to his own house, that he ceased from further solicitation. It was obvious he yet wished to exercise his hospitality: he therefore brought us milk in abundance, and, before I was aware of it, killed and placed before us a kid, most excellently roasted, after their own method, on stones. Seldom was it that we had received similar hospitality from this class, and I was not slow in acknowledging it on this occasion. I learned, as we conversed together in the evening, that amidst the hills he had several flocks, but he preferred remaining here for the purpose of fishing; he had no boat, but caught a sufficiency, either entangled in the shallows or left in the hollows of rocks; vast quantities of fish are also here, as in the Red Sea, thrown up after hard southerly gales.

There were an amazing number of centipedes in this place; we killed fourteen during the evening, and as many on the following morning. Their bite, though painful for the moment, is not considered to be dangerous.

On our way along this sandy belt we passed two date groves, close to the margin of the sea. The trees are nearly overwhelmed with sand. They are said to produce two crops, the one before, the other after the south-west monsoon. My servant, Sunday, in addition to his complaint of the spleen, was now suffering from fever. It was evident the air here was bad; even the slaves were unable to be of service. I had, therefore, not only to prepare my own meals, but to attend them and the camels. Great trouble the latter gave me, because during the several days we remained awaiting the arrival of the ship, I had to lead them, in the heat of the day, a long distance to water. Accustomed on this island to roam over the mountains, feeding on its succulent plants, they, if deprived of them, require water every day. Sandflies, too, and other vermin, were so numerous that we obtained but little rest, and I felt most anxious to return again to the mountains. Our halting-place was about twenty miles from the valley by which we entered the plain; near us was the habitation of an old man, who had occupied for nearly fifty years a cavern beneath the surface of the ground. Wherever limestone rock occurs on the plains, there also it is equally cavernous, with the same formation amidst the hills. No indications are given of your approach to these lonely hermitages; you descend by some rude steps, into what might otherwise appear a well; there you find several apartments, each appropriated to a separate purpose. During my stay I frequently visited my neighbour, who had one wife and two daughters. Although I was received with much hospitality, they always retired when I approached.

Catching a glimpse one day of their interior apartment, I saw, suspended by a string from the roof, a young infant wrapped in a came-line, forming a rude cradle, which one of the daughters, by swinging, was lulling to repose. Several of these cavernous habitations are spread over the plain; those which are tenanted are widely separated from each other, and there appears amidst the occupants no desire to share each other's society, all appearing to isolate themselves with their families. Turtle at certain seasons frequent this part of the island, and ambergris is also found in large quantities; formerly, portions of this substance were substituted for coin, and it yet with the traders bears a proportionate value.

On the 17th, I discovered the ship beating up to the point; but in the evening she anchored so far from the shore, that it was impossible for her to distinguish any signals which I could make. For three days the breeze blew with great violence, and, tired at length with waiting, I entrusted a letter to our neighbour, who promised to deliver it by the first boat which should land there. Not sorry to quit this most desolate tract, I again retraced my steps towards the eastward. A sloping plain ascends two-thirds the height of the mountains which gird the shore: above that the range rises perpendicularly, its height varying from 500 to 800 feet.

Striking off from the sea-coast, along one of the numerous valleys by which this part of the country is crossed, we followed the course of a clear and sparkling stream, passing on our route several hamlets; and, after ascending by a succession of passes, we again found ourselves, on the third day, February 20th, breathing the pure air of the mountains. Near our halting-place there was but one house, tenanted by an old man of most patriarchal appearance, from whom we received much civility. Our fare during this tour was plentiful, though it rarely varied. Bread we had none; rice, with mutton or kid, formed our usual meals. Sometimes we were fortunate enough to obtain fish or dates. The latter are at all times a great luxury, and may be eaten in sickness, when no appetite is felt for other food. In a word, this fruit supplies, in the country where it is found, the want of bread.

On the following day we had heavy rain, and in ascending one of the numerous passes which are found on this part of the island, night overtook us. Cold, wet, and dark, we lost the path several times, and, but for the sagacity of our camels, should have been, more than once, precipitated over the rocks, to the valley below. Although the thermometer was only sixty-two, so completely knocked up were our shivering guides, when we reached the top of the pass, that, after obtaining a glass or two of spirits, and hastily swallowing their evening meal, they wrapped themselves up in all the clothes and mats they could collect, and, paying no attention to their camels, laid themselves down to sleep.

The gale had now increased to a hurricane; vivid lightning flashed over the glens beneath; peals of thunder rolled amidst the mountains; while the torrents were heard rushing down the valley we had just ascended, with a force sufficient to have swept every thing before them. We were fortunate in our halting-place, which was a small cavern, completely sheltering us from the war of the elements.

Sunday and I lighted a large fire, for there was plenty of dry wood in the cave; we dried our clothes, and set to work to cook the supper; but our only cooking-pot was not to be found. Fortune again favoured us; as we were going supperless to bed, Sunday discovered a vessel of earthenware, left by the Bedowins in the cave. In this we made an excellent stew; and after smoking our cigars, and further solacing ourselves with a glass of hot brandy and water, we heeded not the pelting of the pitiless storm without, nor the hardness of our bed within, but slept very soundly until daylight. It was then discovered that our camels, the guides having neglected to tie their legs, had strayed up amidst the mountains, and the whole day was vainly spent in looking for them.

Continuing our journey to the eastward, where our camels were found, the country did not improve in its aspect. Large masses of limestone, ten or fifteen feet in height, with rugged points and level bases, resembling barnacles in form, are found strewn over the plains, which are, moreover, crossed by narrow clefts, of no great depth, their extremities frequently terminating abruptly in a precipice. We passed a small building, which our guides assured me had formerly served as a religious edifice. Near this were several burial-grounds, and a small rude stone seat, on which the Bedowins place their boys, while performing the rite of circumcision.

On the 28th of February we reached the extremity of the high land at Ras Moree, which rises over the low sandy point projecting from beneath to the height of 1,700 feet. On our return towards Tamarida, we witnessed the curious scene represented in the plate which faces this volume. We had continued during the day to pass a succession of these singular habitations. When we first halted no one was visible; but no sooner did our white tent shew itself in the green grass beneath, than the singular conical hill in the foreground became alive with human beings, who came swarming out like ants from an ant-hill. Mr. Cruttenden joined me here.

Continuing our return on the following morning, by a road to the northward of that by which I had reached the cape, we passed one of the most beautiful valleys on the island. It was narrow and thickly wooded, sinking to the depth of 1,400 feet. Down the centre, leaping from rock to rock, rushes a large stream. Two of these cascades have a fall of forty feet; discharging themselves into basins formed by fragments of rocks, and within which the water is clear and pure. On the following day we returned to Tamarida.

soundly u
that our
to tie
mour
in l

## CHAPTER VII.

Ascend the Granite Mountains—Snake—Romantic Scenery—General configuration of the Range—Mortality of Troops—Singular mode of Interment—Ancient Custom.

I HAVE already mentioned that our examination of the island originated in a desire to ascertain if it could be made answerable as a coal depôt; and, if our report was favourable, it was in contemplation to send here a detachment of troops to take possession. Although, from being constantly on the move, neither myself nor any of my party had been seriously indisposed during our tour, yet the reports of the inhabitants induced me to believe that the plain of Tamarida would be found at certain seasons excessively insalubrious. The height of the granite mountains, rising over the town, promised a better climate; I therefore proceeded to ascend them, in order to ascertain how far they were calculated either for a sanatory or a permanent occupation.

After quitting the town, two hours' brisk

walking brought us to the foot of the mountains. The atmosphere was so close and sultry, that I was bathed in perspiration, and received with much thankfulness a bowl of milk which some Bedowins tendered to me. Imagining that I should suffer from the cold as much as themselves, they laughed at the idea of my passing several days there, and predicted that the morrow would again find me on the plains. I gladly, however, accepted the offer of two of their number, who offered their services to act as guides, and to carry the tent, which had been brought thus far on the back of a camel.

We ascended by Wadf Aïuf, a precipitous and rugged glen, very narrow, and thickly wooded. The soil was a rich dark loam, nourishing a great variety of beautiful flowers. After two hours' hard fagging, climbing in many places, and holding on by the roots and branches of trees, we halted about three P. M. under rocks. A few minutes before we did so, I was very nearly bitten by a snake, which the natives call *java*, and the bite of which, they say, proves mortal in the course of a few hours. It had, apparently, just gorged a bird, or some reptile; for it was lying in a half torpid state, partially coiled round the branch of a tree, which in colour it so closely resembled, that, though my hand was nearly touching the head, I did not distinguish it. Sunday, more quick-sighted, did so, and drew my hand hastily away, as it was rearing its head. We killed him. It is singular, that much as my wanderings put me in the way of meeting with snakes, and numerous as they are described to be on this island, yet this is the only occasion on which I have been put so nearly in contact with them.

What a delightful and grateful change, from the over-heated and sultry atmosphere below, to the coolness and invigorating freshness of these regions! Seating myself on the verge of a precipice overlooking the valley, I gazed on the scene around. Every object, after being so long accustomed to the naked arid scenery of Arabia, was novel and interesting. I have travelled much amidst the mountain scenery of that country, of Persia, and of India; but that of Socotra, in wildness and romantic grandeur, surpasses them all.

The sun, at this early period of the day, was sinking beneath the western mountains, and their shadows already obscured the lower portions of the glen. The clustering foliage, clothing portions more elevated, was yet warmed by its golden beams, which were partially obscured by the trees under which I was seated. These, agitated by the wind, threw their chequered shadows and variegated lights around me; while many and beautiful tints illumined the rugged and pinnacled summits of the naked granite spires which tower above all.

On the opposite side of the glen, a clear and sparkling stream held its wild and sportive course; here peeping forth from beneath the foliage, glowing and quivering in the sunbeams; there hurrying forward to lose itself for a brief space in the clear blue pool beneath. On that craggy pinnacle above, where at this distance it appears difficult to conceive that the foot of man could have found a resting-place, is perched a shepherd, his figure standing forth in bold relief against the blue vault of heaven. His voice alone breaks the stillness of the scene; the peculiar shrillness rendering it distinguishable from afar; while his flocks, in obedience to his call, are perceived wending their serpentine course, down the almost perpendicular face of the mountain.

When daylight had ceased to soften the picture, I rejoined Sunday, who was busily employed cooking, after the Socotran manner, a kid, which a Bedowin but a few minutes before had brought him. The bones were first removed, and the whole mass was then thrown into an earthen pot; some rice, in addition to this, formed an excellent meal, to which the whole party sat down. Sunday and myself at first, with the advantage of our knives, held the lead, but were soon compelled to relinquish it; our best efforts were but puny compared to those of our rivals, who did not desist until they had cleared the board. The capacity of these islanders in such matters is prodigious, and they often expressed surprise at the far smaller quantity of food which sufficed us.

In the evening I accompanied the new comers to their cave, which was situated but a short distance from the mountains. Abundance of fuel was at hand, and a blazing fire soon reared its cheerful flames before us. As these rose, red, flickering, and in fantastic wreaths, to the roof, they lighted up a wild and romantic scene. The irregular surface of the projecting masses in the interior of the cave stood forth in bold relief; while the lofty arched roof and numerous caverns, more retiring and remote, were lost in the deepest gloom. Nor was the interest of the scene lessened by the appearance of my companions, whose half-naked figures, plaited hair, and peculiarly marked and expressive countenances, were also in savage keeping with the rest of the picture.

By means of Arabic we were enabled to converse with them; and I was most anxious to ascertain, now we had been so long on the island, and they had also frequently encountered parties belonging to the ship, what they thought of the English, contrasted with other visitors who occasionally arrive at the island. Their reply was a very simple one: "You always pay for what you receive, and never maltreat us or our females, as the pilgrims and others who have touched here did before you; so that we, who at first always fled at your approach, now no longer do so, but bring our sheep, as you have witnessed this evening, and eat them with you."

A charge has been brought against the English, that they are imperious and repulsive in their demeanour towards the Asiatics, and are consequently hated by them. This is one of those sweeping clauses which sounds high, and has just enough of truth in it to allow of its occupying the attention, until we reason or examine the grounds for such an assertion. No European can be wholly liked in the East; both the Hindu and the Mahomedan religion forbid it. But, let it be asked, what other nation has been more successful than ourselves? The Dutch, the Portuguese, the French, were severally in power in India. Were they then loved more than ourselves; or are they now, at Java, Manilla, or Algiers?

Had the English been in possession of the latter city as long as the French, I think our relations with the Bedowins who surround it would have been different, and that we should have been enabled to have shewn ourselves beyond the walls, without the certainty of being shot at from every bush.

Admit that the manners of my countrymen are not the most bland and conciliatory in the world—to what high moral attributes and principles are we to ascribe the superior regard and consideration, which it would be useless to deny, an Englishman enjoys in these countries over most other foreigners.

"I observe this difference between an Englishman and any other Frank," remarked a merchant to me once in Cairo; "I believe the word of the former, and I do not believe that of the latter. When another Frank owes me money, I am anxious to get it paid; for I am convinced he will not do so until he is absolutely obliged. With an Englishman, on the contrary, I feel no anxiety; for he seeks me out, and seems uncomfortable until the debt is paid."

I give the remark precisely in the words in

which it was made to me, and the reader will exercise his own judgment as to the merits of its application. We may laugh at Englishmen squandering their money in other parts of the world; but it is not inconsistent, considering their relative positions there, with oriental notions in these countries.

After remaining talking with this simple people until a very late hour, I returned to the rock under which I had first encamped. Sunday wrapped himself in his cloak, and was soon asleep. It was a lovely evening; the moon "hung imminent," and shed its flood of splendour over the naked spires above, and wooded glens beneath; not a breath of wind was stirring. Wearied with the events of the day, I spread my cloak on a rock, and slept without interruption throughout the night. Refreshed by the purity of the mountain air which I had breathed in my slumbers, I arose at an early hour, and, after bathing in one of the clear and sparkling pools below, I continued my journey up the mountain.

The foliage was, if possible, more dense than at the lower part of the glen, and I had still considerable difficulty in some places to make my way; in others the path led along the brow of a precipice, and was partially cleared for the convenience of the cattle which occasionally cross over this part of the mountain. The morning air was keen and cold, and impregnated with many agreeable odours from the numerous aromatic shrubs and flowers which grew around. Rock doves and other feathered choristers added their wild and plaintive airs to the tinkling of numerous streams, or the hoarser cadence of some louder and more distant fall.

At an elevation of four thousand feet we arrived at a sunny sloping plain, verdant as an English meadow, where several sleek cows were feeding around. The day was clear and cloudless, and we obtained a magnificent view of the greater part of the island, although we had not attained the highest point of the range; for a ridge four hundred feet more elevated was behind us. Yet, as this appeared well adapted for my purpose, I selected a spot which was in some measure sheltered by an impending rock. Here I pitched my tent, and resolved for the present to make it my head-quarters. I found, however, before I had been here long, that the wind swept over the mountains with such violence, that a tent was wholly useless; and I determined, therefore, to employ a few of the natives, to collect stones, and build a rude hut similar to their own. By the next day I had a very snug little room about six feet square; and the tent spread outside, prevented the wind from finding its way through the crevices. I passed my time very delightfully here: I had nothing to do but to wander forth during the day, collect flowers, sketch, or take my gun.

The Jebel Hadjar, or rocky mountains, are a tract of country about ten miles in length, and eleven in breadth. They expose a number of sharp parallel ridges, crossed by steep valleys; and to the northward, the side we ascended, they are more precipitous than on the southern. Above the crest, a saddle, crossed by these valleys, the range runs into rugged and pointed peaks, at very unequal elevations. They are sometimes connected by plateaux of limestone, which is in many instances covered with a very fine soil, producing a luxuriant vegetation, and which might be cultivated to any extent. Many of the valleys would be found equally fertile. Water every where abounds; and, in a word, the industry of a few seasons would here produce, not only the necessaries, but many of the luxuries of life, including, I believe, every fruit common to India, Arabia, or Persia.

It is unnecessary to say much regarding the climate. In the mornings and evenings the transitions from heat to cold on these mountains are very sudden; but during the day the thermometer range is very limited. In the morning the air continues very cool until the sun rises over the summit of the eastern mountains; at noon, provided there was no wind, which was rarely the case, the heat of the sun was very considerable; but the instant it sank beneath the western portion of the range, the air again became cool. In a house of course these variations would be of less amount, and the station we occupied received the sun's rays but for a brief period.

During our stay, I found here, and in other places which I visited on the range, that a superior current of air frequently sweeps down from the higher points, in a direction quite contrary to the prevailing wind below, which would sink the thermometer several degrees. It must, however, be observed that the climate, besides being subject to these variations, was not free from the usual disagreeable accompaniment of highland regions. The summits of the lofty peaks obstruct the clouds, so that from sunshine and clear weather a few seconds bring dense fogs and drizzling rain. Yet these are mere trifles, and are more than compensated for by the clear, pure, and unclouded atmosphere which we enjoy at other times. The nights are, if possible, more pure than the days, and the moon's rays, reflected from the smooth and grey surface of the granite, produce an effect I have rarely seen equalled.

The degree of humidity which was exhibited after sunset, and before sunrise, was also very considerable; our tent in the morning was usually found wet to saturation, and the grass and bushes were every where dripping with moisture; it was impossible for some hours to move without getting completely drenched.

I may here, in the hope they may prove of service to the tyro in travelling, give insertion to a few remarks which suggested themselves to me.

There are several methods of ascertaining the mean temperature of mountain regions, of which the most common are:

1st. Supposing the heat to decrease at certain rates as we advance above the level of the sea.

2dly. By the temperature of copious springs.

3dly. By long continued observations of the barometer.

Mine were taken at nine hours thirteen minutes, A.M., which by vol. x. of the Edinburgh Philosohical Transactions, is the hour in the morning when the mean animal temperature takes place; the mean daily minimum is a little below five hours, A.M., and the maximum two hours forty minutes.

I had with me Leslie's hygrometer, which Daniel recommends to be used at two hours forty minutes. This instrument I need scarcely add was invented by Professor Leslie, and is by some called the thermometric hygrometer, for its use is to work the difference of temperature produced by evaporation. It will be found, however, fully described in the Encyclopedia Britannica.

Considering their extensive utility, I am surprised that we have no well-constructed and portable mountain barometer. On this occasion I had one constructed by Gilbert. It differs from others in the mode of fixing the zero of the scale; a screw attached to the lower portion of the bag raises the surface of the mercury to the point in question. To prevent, however, the frequent accidents which have occurred by the weight of the mercury breaking the tube, the instrument is to be filled at the station where it is required to be used. A glass cistern was affixed to the tube by four steel screws; but the plan does not answer; the screws rusted, the glass cylinders snapped, and the mercury could not be prevented from escaping. I managed, however, to use it for ascertaining the daily variations in the height of the column.

These variations were once supposed to be confined to the vicinity of the equator, but they are now known to extend to every part of the globe, and, according to Humboldt, not only at the level of the sea, but twelve thousand eight hundred feet above it.

The result of my observations and inquiries on this range induced me strongly to recommend it as a station. It is to be regretted that my suggestions were not adopted; for some months after this visit, when the detachment did arrive, they unfortunately encamped in the plain, and were nearly to a man swept off by fevers, as terrific in form and as rapid in progress as those which have made such fell work with our countrymen on the coast of Africa. A second detachment, with more judgment, marched at once to the summit of the mountains, where, until their recal, they enjoyed uninterrupted health; and they described the climate as not inferior to that of Europe.

Formerly the inhabitants of Socotra buried their dead in caves. There are several of these in this vicinity. No coffins appear to have been used; a portion of the cave was walled off, and the corpse then placed at full length within, and covered with a layer of earth, of sufficient thickness to admit of others being placed over it in a similar manner.

One intensely hot day I was strolling along the beach, when my attention was arrested by perceiving something lying there, which an Arab was just leaving. It was an old man stretched on his back, in a hollow scooped out of the sand; nothing but a tattered thin piece of cloth protected him from the fiery heat of the sun's rays; before him were some grain and fragments of half-broiled fish; but he was evidently in the last stage of existence. His companion told me that when a man or woman became unable to work it was customary thus to expose them; food, however, being brought until they expire, when a little earth thrown over them completes their half-formed grave. Such is custom! Yet even this, barbarous as it is, is an improvement on that which formerly was practised.

An old writer, speaking of the inhabitants of Socotra, says that "they generally bury their sick before they breathe their last, making no distinction between a dying and a dead person.

They esteem it a duty to put the patient as soon as possible out of pain, and make this their request to their friends, when they are on a sick bed—which, in all acute disorders, may be called their death-bed. When the father of a family finds himself thus circumstanced, and has reason to believe his dissolution is approaching, he assembles his children round him, whether natural or adopted, his parents, wives, servants, and all his acquaintances, whom he strongly exhorts to a compliance with the following articles of his last will—'never to admit any alteration in the customs or doctrines of their ancestors; never to intermarry with foreigners; never to permit an affront done to them or their predecessors, or a beast stolen from either of them, to go unpunished; and, lastly, never to suffer a friend to lie in pain, when they can relieve him by death.'

"They commonly perform the last request of the dying man by means of a white liquor, of a strong poisonous quality, which oozes from a tree peculiar to this island. Hence it is that legal murders are more common here than in any other country in the world; for, besides the inhuman custom last mentioned, the other requests of dying men produce numberless quarrels, and, by taking revenge of the injuries done to their ancestors, entail family feuds and bloodshed upon their posterity for a long series of years."

Such were the inhabitants of Socotra in the seventeenth century.

## CHAPTER VIII.

Form and Geographical features—Climate—Productions—Dragon's-blood—Natural history—Government—Language—Diseases—Peculiar customs—Religion—Former and present state of the Island contrasted.

I KNOW not a more singular spot on the whole surface of the globe than the island of Socotra. It stands forth, a verdant isle, in a sea girt by two most inhospitable shores; yet its wooded mountains, its glens, its sparkling streams, differ not more from their parched and burning deserts, their bleak and wasted hills, than do its mild and inoffensive inhabitants from the savage and ferocious hordes by which they are traversed. My pursuits and researches were certainly calculated to rouse the suspicion of a bigoted and ignorant people; but the foregoing narrative has shewn how seldom these were interfered with.

Socotra resembles in shape a spherical triangle; its apex being formed by the low sandy point, Ras Moree, lying to the eastward. The whole is a pile of elevated mountains, surrounded by a plain of unequal width; the most central and highest of these rising over Tamarida.

Connected with this group, and extending from north to south, a lower ridge is found, averaging in height about 1,900 feet, and composed of a primitive limestone. From this, hills of similar formation diverge in short ranges to the shore; their outline being mostly smooth, with table summits and rounded sides—except those nearest the sea side, which present a steep wall.

The whole may be considered, therefore, as one mass of primitive rock, and we cannot expect to find it distinguished by any remarkable fertility of soil; I, however, found this so varied that it is difficult to speak of it in general terms. The summits and sides of the greater part of the mountains composing the eastern part of the island, present the smooth surface of the rock entirely denuded of soil; though in some places the rain has worn hollows and other irregularities, in which is lodged a shallow deposit of light earth, from which a few shrubs spring forth.

On the summits of the hills on the northern side of the island, and against the sides and elevated regions in the vicinity of the granite peaks, a dark rich vegetable mould is found, which nourishes a thick and luxuriant vegetation.

In the plain about Tamarida, and some portions near Cadhoop, are several beautiful valleys, such as those I crossed on my return from Ras Moree. The soil there, a reddish-coloured earth, nourishes, at certain seasons, an abundant supply of grass, and appears well adapted for the cultivation of grain, fruit, and vegetables. In the valleys through which the streams flow, not only are there extensive groves of date-trees, but the existence of a broad border of beautiful turf, occasional enclosures of *dukkun,* and, though but rarely, a plantation of indigo or cotton, indicate no want of fertility in the soil. The natives themselves, indeed, are aware of this, and speak of their own indolence in not applying them, as the work of fate.

Though Socotra is situated only a short distance from the continents of Africa and Arabia, and is in fact in the same parallel with their most parched and burning plains, yet, from both monsoons blowing over a vast expanse of of water, it enjoys, at least as compared with them, a remarkably temperate and cool climate. A register of the thermometer, kept in the north-east monsoon, from the 12th of January to the 13th of March, exhibits during that time the mean daily temperature of 70½°; while several streams, at but a short distance from the level of the sea, indicated the mean annual temperature at 74½° (Fahr.). On the hills it is still cooler; and the great elevation of the granite mountains would enable settlers to choose their own climate.

Until a few days before we quitted the island the monsoon blew very fresh, and at times the wind swept through the valleys with a violence which I have rarely seen equalled. The sky was usually overcast; and while in the countries of Asia and Africa, under the same parallel, some time was yet to elapse before the termination of the dry season, Socotra enjoyed frequent and copious rains. This was due to her granite mountains, the lofty peaks of which obstruct the clouds, causing them to deposit their aqueous particles, to feed the mountain streams, or to precipitate themselves in plentiful showers over the surrounding country.

On our second visit, in the south-west monsoon, during the time the vessel remained in

Tamarida Bay, we found the average much higher than the above; but it should not at the same time be forgotten that we were then under the high land on the lee side of the island, and that the wind became heated in its passage across it. On the windward side of the island, the summits of the mountains, and the open part of the coast between Ras Moree and Tamarida Bay, the weather was at this time also delightfully cool.

But though our register was thus affected by local causes, and can be considered as only a partial account of the temperature and state of the atmosphere on the island generally, yet, as a record of the effects of the monsoon at the principal port, it is very valuable. In place of the dark cloudy weather and rain which ushers in this season in India, it was here for the most part clear and cloudless, and the stars at night shone forth with uncommon brilliancy. During this period, also, when it was blowing nearly a hurricane, and when the gusts swept down from the mountains with a force almost irresistible, throwing up the water in sheets, and keeping our decks and masts, to the height of the tops, continually wet with the spray, we had—with the exception of a dense white canopy of clouds formed like the table-cloth over the Table Mountain at the Cape—before the setting in of the breeze with its utmost degree of violence, the same clear and cloudless weather. The wind, when it blew strongest, felt dry; and, indeed, such was its drying quality, that water dropped on the deck evaporated almost instantaneously.

As is usual with winds of this nature, we felt hot or cold, according to the previous state of our skins. If we were perspiring, we felt cool; but otherwise, hot, feverish, and uncomfortable. Notwithstanding the heat of the wind at Tamarida at this season, the natives do not ascribe to it any ill effects. It would merely appear from their testimony, that intermittent fevers are prevalent at the change of either monsoon; and few even of the Arabs from the coast, who reside here any time, escape them.

In the course of my tour I have given some account of the aloe. The production next in importance to that is the gum, dragon's-blood. The trees are not usually met with at a less elevation than eight hundred feet, and they frequently occur as high as three thousand feet above the level of the sea. The trunk, at the height of six feet from the ground, varies from twelve to eighteen inches in diameter, and its height is from ten to twenty feet. The branches are numerous, but short, and thickly intertwined with each other. The leaves are of a coriaceous texture, about twelve inches in length, sword-shaped, and pointed at the extremity; at the base, where they are sessile, they are somewhat extended, and resemble the leaves of the pine-apple. At this part they are connected with the branch of the tree, and, extending from it in an indefinite number, they assume a fan-like shape; several of these together form the upper part of the tree, and their variety in shape and distribution gives rise to most fantastic appearances.

The gum exudes spontaneously from the tree, and it does not appear usual on any occasion to make incisions in order to procure it. Two kinds were shown me; one, of a dark crimson colour, called *moselle*, is esteemed the best, and its price at Muscat is from six to eight rupees the Bengal seer. Dragon's-blood is called by the Arabs, *dum khoheil;* and *edah*, by the Socotrans. I was frequently assured, that not one-tenth of the quantity which might be procured was ever collected by the Bedowins.

As with the aloes, this appears to be consequent on there being no regular demand.

From a tree called, in the language of the island, *amara*, a light-coloured gum is also procured, which is slightly odoriferous, but inferior to that called *oliban*, on the Arabian coast.

Sketches and descriptions were taken of the other varieties of trees on the island; but as they are not suitable for building, or any useful purpose, and are merely remarkable for being indigenous to the island, it does not seem necessary to swell this chapter with a description of them.

Grain is not grown to any extent on Socotra. The millet fields I have noticed in the course of the narrative; they are, however, confined to the eastern part of the island. It is to their date groves, next to their flocks, that the inhabitants look for their principal means of support; though, with the exception of a small one at Colesseah, and another on the west side of the granite peaks, these are also confined to the eastern portion of the island. Here the borders of the numerous streams are lined for miles with them; some being fecundated at the latter end of December, and others as late as the early part of March; by which means they secure to themselves a supply of fresh dates for two months. Those parts of the island which are warmest produce the first crop.

Notwithstanding the large quantities collected from the whole of these groves, the native supply is insufficient for the consumption of the inhabitants, and a large importation takes place annually from Muscat. In the vicinity of Tamarida are some enclosures of beans; and a little tobacco is grown, sufficient for the consumption of the inhabitants.

On the granite mountains some wild orange-trees are found, which produce a sour and bitter fruit. In the language of the island, they are called *tenashur*, and are found in every part of the range, but rarely at a less elevation than two thousand feet above the level of the sea. The Bedowins assert that they continue to bear throughout the year. The fruit clusters very thickly on them; but though equally as fine-looking as the cultivated orange, it never obtains a perfect state. It might, however, prove, as an antiscorbutic, valuable to mariners.

The only esculent vegetables which are found on this range are a species of wild yam, called *foïfut*, which serves the natives, with respect to their other food, as bread does to us. The supply lasts throughout the year, and both the Arab and Bedowin are equally fond of them; and the former bring them from the hills and exchange them with the latter for *jowârree* or dates. They are cooked by being placed on sticks over boiling water. We tried this and several other methods, but found them in all cases much less farinaceous than the yam.

In addition to these, the natives use the roots of several kinds of fern, and other edibles of the same description. They have the *subshâree baïre*, or wild rhubarb, the stalk of which is very palatable; several kinds of sorrel; and a description of water-cress, found on the sea-shore, which boil as well as vegetables.

I have noticed these several productions, because they may prove of service to some vessel hereafter touching there. Whalers sometimes do so, and their crews are not unfrequently suffering from scurvy, for which lime-juice is strongly recommended. The oranges found on these hills form an admirable substitute. But a few days before my arrival on this occasion, one of these vessels, not, in all probability, knowing of the existence of these, had recourse to a method of cure noticed by Dampier, and some of the old buccaneers. The patient, after being stripped, was buried in the bed of a fresh-water stream near the sea-shore, his head alone being left above the surface; in this position he was kept for two hours, and is said to have greatly benefited by the operation.

I have already noticed the fertility of the soil in some places inland, and the extraordinary advantages it possesses in its numerous streams; but both are utterly disregarded by the natives. The whole of the land in the vicinity of the granite peaks is, in the highest degree, susceptible of cultivation; and grain, fruit, or vegetables, to any extent, might be reared in the plains near Tamarida, and amidst the rich valleys in the direction of Ras Moree. The face of the hills on the northern side might be tilled and cultivated in the same manner as is customary in Syria and Palestine. In a word, were it not for the prevailing ignorance and sloth among its inhabitants, Socotra, in a few seasons, might be rendered as celebrated for the extent and variety of its productions, as it is now perhaps remarkable for their small number and little comparative value.

The only animals we saw in Socotra were camels, sheep, asses, oxen, goats, and civet cats. The camels are as large as those of

Syria, but are more remarkable for strength than speed. Continually ascending and descending the mountain passes by bad roads, they become nearly as sure-footed as mules; but, being constantly fed on succulent bushes and herbs, they do not, if this food is taken from them, display the same endurance of thirst as those of Arabia. When confined to the parched shrubs which grow on the low land, they require to be watered daily. Camels are principally used by traders while seeking *ghee*, &c. among the mountains, and by the inhabitants when transporting dates or firewood to and from the interior. The whole number on the island does not exceed two hundred. For those I took with me I paid six dollars per month each. The price for which they are sold is usually from twenty to thirty dollars.

Cows are very numerous near Tamarida, and on the mountains in its vicinity. They are usually of the same colour as that which distinguishes the Alderney breed in England; but their size does not exceed that of the small black Welsh cattle. The hump, which marks those of India and Arabia, is not observed here; and they have the dewlap, which is supposed to be a distinguishing feature in the

European cow. The pasturage for them is abundant, and their appearance is consequently sleek and fat; their flesh, when young, is of the most superior quality. The natives keep them mostly for the sake of the milk, with which *ghee*, so much in estimation in Arabia and Africa, is made. They are not, therefore, solicitous to part with them, and the prices which they demand for those in condition is proportionately high; ten dollars were paid for those we purchased. Their flesh was pronounced equal to that of our finest English oxen.

We had reason to believe that bullocks or cows are rarely killed by the people of Socotra, excepting either at the death of some individual possessing a herd of them, or some influential personage. Indeed, so anxious do they appear on these occasions to prevent the possibility of this ceremony being omitted, that I have known them, when any of their family was sick, send for five or six from the mountains, and keep them in readiness for slaughtering the instant that death should take place.

When killed, a portion of the meat is sent to their different neighbours, which is considered as equivalent to requiring the attendance of the individual at the interment of the deceased; and after this is accomplished, the whole party return and feast on the remainder, until it is either consumed or carried away. The hides are tanned, and sent to Muscat for sale. The whole number at present on the island is about sixteen hundred.

My narrative will shew how numerous are the sheep and goats in every part of the island. Amidst the hills over Tamarida, and on the plain contiguous to it, there are a great number of asses, which were described to me as differing from the domestic ass; but after repeated opportunities of observing them, I could find no reason for such a distinction. The introduction of camels having superseded the necessity of employing asses as beasts of burden, they are permitted by their masters to stray where they please, and now wander about in troops of ten or twelve, evincing little fear unless approached very near, when they dart away with much rapidity. Though not applied by the natives to any useful purpose, yet they would no doubt be found serviceable should occasion again require them.

Hyenas, jackals, monkeys, and other animals which are common to the shores of either continent, are unknown here; we do not even find antelopes; a circumstance the more singular, as they abound in the islands off the Arabian coast. Civet cats I have noticed in the course of the narrative. Dogs are also unknown; and one we had on board was frequently mistaken by the natives for a hog. I saw but few snakes during my stay on the island, and the head of these were too much bruised for me to ascertain if they were poisonous, but the natives assured me that such was their character. From them I also learned that, after the rains, a great many make their appearance, and some marvellous stories were told me respecting their size and fierceness.

On the low land we found an astonishing number of scorpions, centipedes, and a large and venomous description of spider, called by the Arabs *nargub*, the bite of which creates alarming inflammation, and even death, with young children. In some parts of the island, on the plains, if a stone was turned over, one or more of these insects was generally found underneath.

Locusts have been rarely seen in Socotra. Ants are very numerous, and the bite of one kind is scarcely less painful than the sting of a wasp. Near the *dukkun* enclosures field-mice are often observed; and on the hills rats and other vermin are common. The cameleon is a native of the island: the natives frequently brought them to me for sale, and some were larger than I had before seen.

The only birds we saw were crows, wild ducks, a species of water-fowl with red legs and dark plumage, wood pigeons, numerous swallows, lapwings, owls, bats, and four different species of vulture; the last particularly useful in clearing the earth of carcases and filth. There is also a small bird, with a red beak and dark purple plumage, called *mahuarad* in the Socotran language, which utters a shrill and loud cry, not unlike that which might be produced by an effort of the human voice.

Cassawaries are said to have been seen on the island, as well as flamingos. I have seen the latter passing over, but never the former.

It has been already noticed, that the government of the island of Socotra was, from a very early period, dependent on the kings of the Incense country; and the early Portuguese navigators found them, on their first arrival, still in the undisturbed possession of their ancient patrimony. When Albuquerque conquered

Tamarida; he vested its government in the hands of some of his officers, who, with a remnant of his troops, were left behind to retain it. But the Portuguese sway was short; they speedily intermarried with the inhabitants, lost their ascendancy, and Socotra again resumed its dependence on its ancient masters.

From this period until within the last half century, a brother, or some near relation, of the Sultan of Kisseen, on the Arabian coast, resided constantly on the island as its governor; but it is now merely subjected to an annual visit from such a personage. The revenue is then collected, and any complaints which require the interference of the Sultan are brought before him.

During our stay at Kisseen and on the island we made numerous inquiries to ascertain who at present exercises such a power; but it proved no easy matter to discover this. The old Sultan being blind, and incapable of managing the affairs of his government, various claimants appeared; but one Abdallah being pointed out as the influential individual, we procured from him the letters which specified the nature of our visit, and required the islanders to render us any assistance we might stand in need of.

As already seen, little attention was, however, paid to these letters; and during our stay another chief, Hamed ben Tary, arrived, and under threat of burning the town, succeeded at Golenseah in procuring a few dollars' worth of *ghee*. He also sent directions to Tamarida, forbidding our being furnished with camels or guide; and again departing for Kisseen, boasted of what he had done.

After him no other member of the family was expected on the island; and as the sum collected annually barely exceeds in value two hundred dollars, the authority of the Sultan may be considered more nominal than real. Abdallah, in his visits, has been known to inflict chastisement with his own hand on the Bedowins who neglected to bring him the full quantity of *ghee* to which he considered himself entitled, and even to imprison them for a few days; but I could not learn that he possessed sufficient power to inflict punishment of any kind on the Arabs, the greater number of whom are indeed exempt from contributions. It is from those who collect *ghee* at Tamarida, Golenseah, and Cadhoop, that he obtains this only article which he at present draws from the island.

The attention of Abdallah during his annual visit is now wholly directed towards this collection of revenue; though complaints from former usage are occasionally brought before him; yet the instances are rare, and his decisions are not much attended to. At Tamarida, an old Arab, our host, named Abdallah, possesses some influence. Another at Golenseah, named Salem, is also qualified by the townsmen with the title of Sheikh, in order, mainly, it would appear, that he may receive presents from vessels visiting the port. But, altogether, nothing is more certain than that they do not possess throughout the island a constituted authority, either civil or military, or of any description whatsoever.

Notwithstanding the singular anomaly of so great a number of people residing together without any chiefs or laws, offences against the good order of society appear infinitely less frequent than among more civilized nations. Theft, murder, and other heinous crimes, are almost unknown; and no stronger instance can be given of the absence of the former, than the fact of my wandering for two months on the island, without having during that period missed the most trifling article. Some intelligent natives, also, assured me that the only disturbances known were occasional quarrels among the Bedowins, respecting their pasture grounds, which were usually either settled by the individuals fighting the matter out with sticks, or by the interference of their friends. It is, no doubt, this security of person and property that has brought so many settlers, from the continents on either side, to the island.

Beyond the patriarchal authority hereafter noticed, there does not appear to be any subordinate rank or distinction; and all are respectable in proportion to their wealth in flocks and herds. That the Socotrans possess no maritime enterprise, is at once shown by their having no boats; yet they do not appear averse to commercial pursuits; and the voyager who may have to transact business with them, will find to his cost, unless he be somewhat wary, that their talents for selling and bartering are not contemptible. The wants of those who reside on the island are, however, so few and so easily satisfied, that they have but little motive to stimulate them to more industrious pursuits; and I question if, under the name and protection of their Arab chiefs (notwithstanding their occasional rapacity), they do not enjoy more liberty and ease in the indulgence of their natural indolence than they would do if placed under more active rulers. The doctrines of the Koran, which are widely and generally disseminated amongst them, are not calculated to remove their apathetic habits.

The inhabitants of the island may be divided into two different classes: those who inhabit the mountains, and the high land near the western extremity of the island—who, there is every reason to believe, are the aborigines; and those who reside in Tamarida, Golenseah, Cadhoop, and the eastern end of the island. The latter are a mongrel race, the descendants of Arabs, African slaves, Portuguese, and several other nations.

Of the former, or Bedowins, I shall give as full a description as my materials will admit; premising, however, that although from personal observation I have been enabled to procure every necessary information connected with the present physical habits and domestic manners of this isolated race, yet on some interesting points connected with their former condition, religion, and usages, I was anxious to obtain some knowledge, but found, from the jealous and suspicious character of those with whom I was obliged to converse, this was nearly impossible: they either declined to answer my questions altogether, or made replies calculated to mislead.

It would appear they are gross idolaters, worshipping the moon, and offering, in times of drought, petitions to her. At the beginning of Lent they make a solemn sacrifice to that luminary, entering their temples also, and performing various ceremonies at its rising and setting. They were also described as going to their burial-places, striking together two pieces of odoriferous wood. This they perform three times a day, and as often at night; after which, putting a large cauldron, suspended by three chains, over a great fire, they dip into it splinters of wood, with which they light their altars and the porch of the temple. They then put up their prayers to the moon, that she will enlighten them with her countenance, shed upon them her benign influence, and never permit foreigners to intermix with them.

They make also an annual procession round the temples, preceded by a cross; and the whole ceremony ends upon the priest's clapping together his hands, as a signal that the moon is tired with their worship. Others say, that the signal consists in cutting off the fingers of him who holds the cross; in recompense for which, he has a stick given him, on which are certain marks, fordding all persons, of whatever rank or condition, ever after to molest or hurt him; on the contrary, they are to aid and assist him with all their power, in whatever manner he might require their help; and they are further doomed to suffer corporal punishment, and the loss of an arm, unless they respect and honour him as a martyr to religion.

The Arabs who visit Socotra, in consequence of the pastoral habits of this class, and their wandering mode of life, bestow on them the appellation of Bedowins; to which race, though they differ widely in some points, yet they have in others a striking resemblance. The principles of their political constitution are exceedingly simple; all are divided into families or tribes, each possessed of a determined domain on the island, and each having a representative or head, who formerly exercised a patriarchal authority over them. In general, the office is hereditary, though it is sometimes filled by persons who have been selected for other reasons.

It was to this individual that the Sultan formerly, when he resided on the island, looked for the collection of his tribute; and to the Sultan he was also in some measure answerable for the good conduct of his tribe; but at present his authority appears to be merely that of an influential individual, before whom complaints are taken for arbitration, but who possesses no power to punish a delinquent.

An individual may also carry his complaint before the Sultan or his deputy, or he may (which is the usual practice) retaliate on the injurer or any member of his family; but these affairs are not carried to the sanguinary length they are in Arabia, where the murder of an individual is revenged on the persons of his assassins or their relatives. I made numerous inquiries, but could not ascertain that their quarrels ever terminated in death to either party; which may, in some measure, be owing to their having neither fire-arms nor weapons of any other description, excepting sticks and stones.

Still, their peaceable habits are forcibly illustrated by the fact of so many tribes occupying territories intermingled with each other, where the valuable nature of pasturage, and the scarcity of water, compel them from different quarters to meet at the same spot without reference to the actual owners; and that yet quarrelling amongst them is of the rarest occurrence.

The men are usually tall, with strong, muscular, and remarkably well-formed limbs, a facial angle as open as that of Europeans, the nose slightly acquiline, the eyes lively and expressive, the teeth good, and the mouth well formed. Their hair is worn long, and curls naturally; but, unlike that of the inhabitants of Madagascar and several of the Asiatic islands, without approach to a woolly or crisp texture. They also generally wear a beard and whiskers, but never moustaches. They have no characteristics in common with the Arabs or Somaulees; and some points about them are even essentially different. Their complexion varies a good deal, some being as fair as the inhabitants of Surat, while others are as dark as the Hindoos on the banks of the Ganges.

They walk with an erect gait over the worst ground, and bound over the hills like antelopes. From constantly climbing the rocks and mountains, they have contracted a habit of turning in their toes, which gives them when on the plains a slight degree of awkwardness in their walk.

Yet, notwithstanding this defect, the regularity of their features, the fairness of their complexions, (for those which are dark are but a small portion of their number,) and the models of symmetry which they occasionally present to the eye, render them a remarkably good-looking people, distinct and removed from any of the varieties of the human race seen on the shores of the continent on either side.

Their dress consists of a piece of cloth wrapped round the waist, with the end thrown over the shoulders, but without ornaments. In their girdle is placed a knife; and they carry in their hands a large stick. In their various modes of dressing the hair they display a little foppery; some having it frizzled, like that of the Bisharee Arabs on the coast of Egypt; others allowing it to curl naturally; while the greater number permit it to grow to a considerable length, and plait it into tresses, confined to the head by a braided cord made from their own hair. Their skins are clear, shining, and remarkably free from eruptive or cutaneous disorders. Many, however, appear scarred, from the application of hot irons, for the removal of local complaints—a mode of cure they are as fond of practising as are their neighbours the Arabs of the continent.

The same remarks may be applied with little alteration to the persons and features of the females. We find in them the same symmetry of form, the same regularity of feature, and the same liveliness of expression; but their complexion does not vary in an equal degree, few being darker than the fairest of the men, and some, especially when young, being remarkably pretty. The legs of many advanced in age are of an astonishing thickness; but this defect is chiefly observable among those who reside in the low lands, and seldom occurs among the highland females. Their dress consists of a camaline* bound round their waist by a leathern girdle, and a kind of wrapper of Dungaree cloth, which is thrown over their shoulders. Round their necks they wear necklaces made of red coral, coloured glass, amber, with sometimes a string of dollars to each ear; they wear also three, and sometimes four, ear-rings, made of silver, and about three inches in diameter; two are worn on the upper, and one on the lower part of the ear. They go unveiled, and converse freely with the other sex.

I have frequently had occasion to remark, in the course of the narrative, the singular cavern-

* A coarse woollen cloth, manufactured and used in Arabia.

ous habitations, which the bounty of providence, in the numerous hollows amidst the mountain ranges, has bestowed on these islanders. The rocks here, wherever limestone occurs, are equally cavernous with the hills. A cave is accordingly selected, of which they widen, if necessary, the entrance, so as to allow it to open into an enclosure; the upper part is then covered over with rafters, on which turf and some earth is placed, so that it becomes difficult at a short distance to distinguish it from the surrounding country; and a wall of loose stones encloses a circular space, about thirty yards in diameter, in the immediate vicinity, which serves at night as a fold for their sheep and goats. I visited the interior of several of these. The only furniture they contained was a stone for grinding corn, some skins on which to sleep, other skins for holding water and milk, some earthen cooking pots, and a few camelines* hanging on lines tied across the roof. In one of these, tied by the four corners, and suspended from a peg by a string, will frequently be seen a child sleeping; and this contrivance serves also as a cradle, being swung to and

* Camlet or camelot, a woollen cloth, supposed to be made of camels' hair.

fro when they wish to compose its tenant to sleep.

In hot weather, when the ground is parched with heat, these caves are of a clammy coldness. The Bedowins are by no means particular in keeping them clean; and they usually swarm with fleas and other vermin. The mildness of the climate renders a fire-place unnecessary, and the fire which is required for culinary purposes is lighted outside. The closeness of the interior, as they have no other opening than the door, would otherwise, I believe, be intolerable.

## CHAPTER IX.

Occupation of Men and Women—Process of Ignition—Bedowin Cheerfulness—Modes of Salutation—Language—Numerals—Diseases—Traditions—Mixed Population—Religion—Island, how peopled—Conclusion.

The men pass their time in tending their flocks, in collecting dragon's-blood and aloes, and in occasional visits to the towns, where the two latter productions, with *ghee*, are exchanged for dates, *dhorra*,* and clothes. Accustomed to traverse their mountains from childhood, they perform on such occasions journeys of thirty or forty miles, climbing almost perpendicular precipices, and crossing deep ravines, without apparently experiencing any fatigue or inconvenience.

The principal employment of the females abroad is looking after the flocks; at home they make *ghee*, card and spin wool, which they afterwards weave into camelines, and attend to

* *Holcus sorghum*, or *Sorghum vulgare*. Sorgo is an Italian word; dhurrah, or dhorrah, being the Egyptian term.

their domestic duties; in addition to which, as with most other barbarous nations, much of the toil consequent on their pastoral mode of life falls principally on them; and I have frequently seen the wives at the close of the day, after securing their flocks, proceed, with their children on their backs, a distance of several miles, to fill and bring home skins of water, while their husbands have remained with no other occupation than smoking or sleeping.

They have a curious method of cleaning their wool. They place it in a heap on the floor, and hold a bow over it, the string of which they snap against it, till all the dust has flown off. Their method of weaving is also very simple, but a description of it without a figure would be unintelligible.

As it is difficult for them to procure steel, they have recourse to a method of obtaining combustion, practised by several savage nations. They procure two pieces of wood, the one hard (nebek if procurable), the other a short flat lath from a date branch. The former is twelve inches long, and is inserted in a hollow formed for the purpose in the latter. The stick is then twirled briskly between the two palms, pressing it at the same time with some force, until the dust ground out by the attrition (and which escapes down the side by a small groove) ignites; it is then placed on a palm branch, and flame is produced.

The Bedowins subsist chiefly on milk, and on the grain and dates which they receive in exchange for their *ghee*. When occasion calls for a feast, or a visitor arrives, a goat or sheep is killed. Their mode of cooking is very simple. They separate the meat from the bones, cut it into small pieces, and boil the whole in an earthen pot. They use no dishes, and the meat is placed on a small mat, round which they sit. In eating, contrary to the usual Mussulman custom, they cut their meat with knives, which are procured from whalers and other vessels that touch at the island.

The moral character of these Socotran Bedowins stands high; and the rare occurrence of heinous crimes among them has been already noticed. In general, they may be considered as a lively, generous race; but the most distinguishing trait of their character is hospitality, which is practised alike by all, and is only limited by the means of the individual called on to exercise it. Nor is this, as with the Socotran Arabs, confined to those of their own faith; and while with the latter we were unceasingly tired by silly questions, relating either to our religion or our views on the island, the Bedowins gave themselves no concern either about the one or the other. Ever cheerful, they were always ready to enter into conversation, or to be pleased with what was shown them. I saw no instrument of music during our stay on the island, but they appear passionately fond of song; and on one occasion, at a wedding, I saw them, as has been noticed in the narrative, engaged in dancing.

The Bedowins have a great variety of modes of salutation. Two friends meeting will kiss each other on the cheek or shoulder six or eight times, then shake hands, kiss them, and afterwards interchange a dozen sentences of compliment. They have also the same singular and awkward mode of salutation which is practised at Kisseen, where they place their noses together, and accompany the action by drawing up their breath at the same time through the nostrils audibly. Male and female relations, in public, salute each other in this manner. Those of different sexes, who are merely acquaintances or friends, kiss each others shoulder, except in the case of the principal individual of the tribe, whose knees the females salute, while he returns the compliment on their forehead. The old men salute children in the same manner.

I am not sufficiently versed in oriental literature, to ascertain what affinity the Socotran language may bear to the Arabic, or to any African language; I have therefore subjoined in the Appendix a vocabulary of words in most general use among the Bedowins, by which I trust the scholar may be able to proceed in an inquiry that can scarcely fail to lead to interesting results. I may notice, in passing, that the mountaineers from the Arabian coast are sometimes able to make themselves well understood by the Bedowins of Socotra; but the Arabs from Muscat, or from any of the neighbouring towns, are quite unable to do so.

The Socotran language is in general use even by those who have permanently settled on the island; and Arabic is only spoken by the merchants when transacting business with the traders who arrive in their buggalows.

At as late a period as when the Portuguese visited Socotra they found on it books, written in the Chaldean character.* I hoped conse-

* The Ethiopic was commonly called *Chaldean* in the sixteenth century. Vide Adelung's Mithridates, vol. i. p. 407. The people of Socotra were Christians at that time.

quently to be able to procure some manuscripts or books which might serve to throw light on the history of the island; but in answer to repeated inquiries regarding such, I was always assured that some, which they acknowledged to have possessed, they left in their houses when they fled to the hills, and that the Wahabees, during their visit, destroyed or carried them off. The former is the most probable, as these sectaries, in the genuine spirit of Omar's precept, value only one book.

With the use of the compass the Bedowins are totally unacquainted; and they have no terms in their language by which to express the cardinal points. The superiority of the Arabic numerals over their own has induced them entirely to discontinue the use of the latter, and in all transactions among themselves, as well as with the Arabs, the former are now used. The numerals are given in the Appendix, but in the decimal manner which was adopted they could not advance farther than ten hundred; and I have frequently inquired, without success, for some term to express a thousand. This gives no very high opinion of their mental capacity, and it furnishes, unless they have sadly retrograded, a strong proof also of their never having made any considerable progress in civilization.*

During my stay in Socotra I saw but few cases of illness. Four of cancer, and as many of elephantiasis, were brought to me for medical assistance. A hard and painful swelling of the abdomen, brought on by irregularity in diet, was frequent; but this was not surprising, as a Bedowin will live for several days on milk and a little *dukkun*,† and then feast to excess on a sheep, the flesh of which is but half boiled. Some bad sores were shown me, occasioned by punctures from the thorns of the nebek;‡ but in general diseases are of very rare occurrence, and the Bedowins may be considered a hardy and healthy race. In the most solitary and lonely ravines and valleys I occasionally met with idiots, who were permitted to stray about by themselves. Food is given them when they approach any habitation; but they usually

* The resemblance between some of those words given in the Appendix, and the Arabic, is very striking; but in looking over the vocabulary, the proximity of the island to the continents on either hand must not be forgotten, as it may have given rise to a variety of words and usages common to them, though the people may otherwise have ever remained distinct.

† Dhokn, or dokn; i. e. *Sorghum sarcharatum*—the Dáb-d'hán of the Hindús.

‡ *Rhamus*, or *Zizphus*—*Lotus*, or *Spina christi*.

subsist either on the wild herbs, which they gather on the mountains, or on the wild goats, which they knock on the head with stones. Near Ras Moree I saw one of these men going about perfectly naked. I came on him unexpectedly, but he fled with much celerity the instant he saw me.

Of the many peculiar customs which existed before the introduction of Mahomedanism, a few only are now retained, of which the most singular is, that they do not circumcise their children until they are past the age of puberty; while with other Mahomedans this is performed at a very early age. On the eastern part of the island, amidst the mountains, I was shown a rude stone chair, in which it is customary for the Bedowins to seat their youths (who are sometimes brought from a long distance) while the operation is performed.

They have preserved the remembrance of a singular trial by ordeal formerly practised. An individual supposed to have been guilty of any heinous crime was placed, bound hand and foot, on the summit of some eminence, and there compelled to remain three days. If rain fell during that period on or near him, he was considered guilty, and punished by being stoned to death; but if the weather, on the contrary, continued fair, he was acquitted.

They are, in the more remote parts of the island, said to still retain the custom of transferring their own progeny to another person. During pregnancy, it is left at the will of the mother, that the father may give the child away as soon as it makes its appearance in the world. If her consent is obtained, a fire is lighted before the door of their cave, to denote his intention, and the child, as soon as born, is sent to another family, in which it is brought up with every tenderness and attention. Children reared under this singular custom retain through life the title of "children of smoke." It is common for a father who thus exposes his own, to receive in a similar manner the offspring of another of his tribe.

Burckhardt tells us that the scheriffs of the Hedjaz have a nearly similar custom. After the first five or six days the child, if a boy, is transferred to another tribe, and the mother is not permitted again to see him until he attains to man's estate. In this manner Mahommed their prophet was reared.

Some other popular traditions were related to me, but they appeared so little peculiar or characteristic as scarcely to be worth transcription. They have a story that there is a class of women who, like the Gouls of Arabia, lie in ambush in lone and secret places, to catch and devour the weary traveller; and so prevalent is this belief, that I have heard both Arabs and Bedowins maintain that a greater number of deaths occurred in this than in any other way. The gravity indeed with which such opinions were maintained, even by the more enlightened of the natives, surprised me a good deal; neither ridicule nor argument had any effect in shaking their faith. The probable origin of these tales is, that bodies of the mountaineers fall occasionally from the rocks, and are sometimes found to be partly devoured by vultures and other birds of prey: the love of the horrible and marvellous fills up the rest of the story.

It may appear singular that while the population of the eastern part of the island is mixed and varied, that of the western still continues pure. The cause is this: the want of water, felt during the greater part of the year on this part, and its general sterility, offer so little inducement to the native Arabs to reside there, that, with the exception of some fishing hamlets, I did not, in my journeying in that part, meet half-a-dozen families.

The Bedowins make no scruple to give their daughters to the native Arabs, and even to visiters who may pass but a short time on the island. These, departing with their husbands, their sons naturally follow the avocation of their fathers, and rarely, if ever, return to the pastoral pursuits of their maternal progenitors; while the females again are not married to Bedowins; for the Arabs, though they have no objection to take a Bedowin wife, would hold themselves disgraced were they to marry their daughters to any but those of their own class.

Of those who are comprehended under the name of Bedowins, there are a few distinct tribes of which it is necessary that separate mention should be made. Those most worthy of attention are a small tribe, of about one hundred and fifty men, called Beni Rahow, in the vicinity of Ras Moree. Their forefathers are said to have been Jews, and the features of the tribe still retain a strong resemblance to those of that race. Some others, known under the general appellation of Camhane, are said to be descended from the Portuguese; but I think this very doubtful. They occupy the granite mountains, are rich in flocks of sheep and cows, and though the resemblance to the European cast of countenance may still be traced, and in some cases they have even preserved their original name, yet they exhibit none of those symptoms of physical degradation which are observable in the race of Portuguese in India; on the contrary, some of the finest figures and most intelligent people I saw on the island were of this class. Though readily recognized by the other tribes, their descent appears in no way to be considered as a reproach to them. It was said that a few families in the mountains continued to speak even their original language, but I never fell in with any such. Some of the hills on the east and north side of the island still, however, retain the appellations bestowed upon them by Portuguese.

As I have preserved the name of Bedowin, bestowed on the mountain-tribes, I shall also retain the name of Arabs, with which the remainder have invested themselves. Under this designation, are included those who occupy Tamarida, the villages of Cadhoop and Golenseah, and the greater part of the eastern portion of the island. They may all be classed as foreigners, or the descendants of foreigners who have settled there. The principal part are Arabs, left by boats passing between Zanzebar and the Arabian coast, who marry and remain permanently; a few others are Indians, Somaulis, Arabian slaves, &c. attracted hither by various motives. All preserve the recollection of their original country, and for this purpose subjoin its name to their own. Thus our guide was called Suleiman Muscaty, or Suleiman from Muscat.

Though so mixed a class, the Socotra Arabs all wear the same dress, and have adopted the same language and customs. Their colour, features, and figure, as may be expected, are so varied that it is impossible to speak of them in any general terms; they have, in fact, every grade, from the flattened nose, thick lip, and woolly head of the negro, to the equally well-known characteristics of the Arabs. Their dress consists of a loose single shirt, descending below the knees, confined to the waist by a leathern girdle, to which are suspended all the arms they can muster. The lower classes wear nothing but a piece of striped linen, with another, when they are exposed to the sun, thrown over their shoulders. In rainy or cold weather they all wear a thick woollen coat, sufficiently large completely to envelop them. The female dress consists of a long chemise of Indian cloth, with a loose wrapper over it, the ends of which, being drawn round their person, are brought up to the neck, in order to serve as a veil, when they desire to conceal their face.

The employments of this class are either tending their date-groves and flocks, making ghee, or trading between Muscat and Zanzebar. Their date-groves give them but little trouble; for as soon as the owner can scrape together enough money, he buys a slave to attend upon them; and if his wealth increases, he adds to the number both of slaves and trees. Traders proceed among the mountains on camels, taking with them various articles, which they exchange for ghee; the quantity collected is very great; I was assured that in some seasons it amounts to 2,500 measures. Those who trade to Zanzebar with this article receive in exchange for it grain and slaves. The Socotran Arabs treat their slaves with great harshness; they work them hard, and feed and cloth them but indifferently. Their numbers are fast increasing, as the climate agrees well with them; and, conscious of this, they have recently manifested an inclination to rebel.

Commercial pursuits can only be engaged in during the fair or north-east monsoon, and it follows that a considerable portion of their time is passed without employment of any kind; to obviate the tedium of which period, I did not observe that they have recourse to games of chance or public amusement of any description. Their time appears spent in visiting each other, drinking coffee, smoking and sleeping. In place of taking up their abodes in caves, as the Bedowins do, the Arabs who reside in the country live in huts, which are mostly of a circular form, the walls being constructed of loose stones, and cemented with mortar, of which mud is the principal ingredient. They are rarely more than four feet high, inclosing a space from twelve to fourteen feet diameter. The roof is with some flat, and with others conical; they plaster the upper part of this to the sides, constructed of the branches of date trees, and in order to prevent the rain getting through.

In several of those which I visited it was impossible to stand upright. Fleas and other vermin swarmed in these wretched habitations, not larger than an English pigstye, in which two or three families, each consisting of four or five individuals, resided. It is not therefore surprising that fever sometimes sweeps off a whole hamlet. Were the materials of which these wretched and unseemly buildings are constructed scarce, and only to be procured with difficulty, we might pardon the little attention to comfort, accommodation, or health, which their construction exhibits; but when these are abundant, and there are better models in the town before them, that they are thus indifferently lodged, furnishes a strong proof of their sloth and indolence, and, with many other circumstances, may be considered as showing that they have little capacity or inclination for improvement.

Though the Bedowins are healthy, the Arabs seem a weak and sickly race. Dangerous fevers prevail among them after the rains, and the graves in the vicinity of Tamarida are frightfully numerous; so that it may be truly said of that town, that it contains treble the number of houses than it does of inhabitants, and ten times the number of tombs than it does of both. On other parts of the island, wherever vestiges of former habitations could be traced, there might also be seen the same proportion of graves. The Arabs formerly paid great attention to their tombs. One stone was placed at the head, another at the feet, and a third in the centre; and on the first were inscribed the name, age, &c. of the deceased. But the Wahábees, from their aversion to any kind of decoration over the remains of the dead, during their stay broke and destroyed the whole of those which they could reach.

My attention was particularly directed towards obtaining information respecting the forms of religion of these islanders. At present every individual on the island is, or professes himself to be, a Mussulman; but the Bedowins, as in Arabia, hold their tenets but loosely. Many neglect the fast of the Ramazan, and few are acquainted with morning and evening prayers—those few rarely troubling themselves with repeating them. Circumcision, as already noticed, is not practised until a late period, and in some families I have reason to believe it is omitted altogether. The Socotran Arabs, on the contrary, are zealous professors of the Mussulman faith, though at the same time utterly ignorant of its most essential doctrines; and, like all those nations who possess but a slight knowledge of their tenets, they are bigoted and intolerant to an insufferable degree.

The Mahara Arabs, from the coast of Arabia,

a noble race, who occasionally reside on the island for a few months, ridicule them for this spirit of intolerance, and assured us, even in the presence of the zealots, that the Socotrans were poor wretches, who had nothing to plead in defence of their bigotry, save the lowest state of ignorance, and their mongrel descent. After the receipt of Ahmed-ben-Tary's letter, prohibiting our further progress through the interior of the island, and when I was confined by the Socotran Arabs for several days in the town, it was principally through the influence of the Mahara Arabs, exercised on that occasion, joined to Abdallah's roguery, that I was again enabled to set forward on my journey. The behaviour of the former on all similar occasions exhibited a mixture of irresolution, timidity, and avarice, which I have never seen equalled. They wavered between dread of the sheikh, if they permitted us to go, and fear of missing what they might gain if they prevented us, by hiring out their camels. Exorbitant demands were thus made; and when they found I would not listen to these, they continued to hold councils for three days, during which I had all packed up in readiness for starting. Permission was given and refused more than half a dozen times.

It is observed by Malte Brun, in his 'Universal Geography,' that the population of this island might form a subject of lengthened discussion. He notices, on the authority of Philostorgius, Edrisi, and Hamdoullah, that a colony, sent by Alexander the Great, remained here for a long period; that during the time of Philostorgius (an ecclesiastical historian, who wrote a history of the Church, on Arian principles, at the conclusion of the fourth century), they spoke the Syriac language: and he cites various other authorities to prove the existence of a race of Christians by whom the island was peopled until as late a period as 1593, when the Nestorians and Jacobites had each a bishop residing on it. Even when Sir Thomas Roe visited it in 1612, he observes, "that the Bediognes," as he styles them, "where of the Nestorian persuasion."

As the channel of the Indian trade, at the early period to which this author refers, was by way of Socotra and the ports in the Red Sea, it is not so extraordinary that Christianity should have been thus early established here.

Mr. Sale observes, in his "Preliminary Discourse," that the persecutions and disorders which happened in the Eastern Church soon after the beginning of the third century, obliged great numbers of Christians to seek shelter in the country of liberty (Arabia); who being for the most part of the Jacobite community, that sect generally prevailed among the Arabs." And although it does not appear that the southern parts of the peninsula were subject to the ecclesiastical rule of either the Nestorian or Jacobite bishops, yet, from the circumstances above adverted to, it is not probable that they would have overlooked a spot like Socotra, where there is every reason to believe they could indulge unmolested in the open profession of their faith. With respect to the disappearance of these primitive Christians, as well as those, if any, which where left on the island by the Portuguese, it may be observed that it would be strange, surrounded as they were by natives universally professing the Mussulman religion, and receiving no fresh influx from those of their own persuasion, if they had not merged into the principles of their Arab masters. That this was accomplished gradually, and not by any violent or exterminating measures, appears evident by their descendants being considered a distinct race to the present day. That numerous colonies, of different nations or persuasion, formerly existed on the island, is evident, from the present arrangement and distribution of its inhabitants into tribes, many of which are still recognized as of foreign origin.

Time has not produced a greater change in the government or condition of this island than it has in its ecclesiastical arrangement. In place of one archbishop and two bishops, there is now but a single priest, who combines in his own person the various offices of moollah, muezzin, and schoolmaster. A single cadi solemnizes the whole of the marriages which take place throughout the island; and I have, on more than one occasion, met Bedowins seeking him for a certificate, when he has been about on the hills cultivating his date-groves. Two small and insignificant mosques at Tamarida, and one yet smaller at Golenseah, are now the only places of worship for the reception of the faithful. What form of religion the establishment of the Christian faith displaced, would form a curious subject of inquiry. A ruinous building was shown me, which was said to have been an ancient place of worship; but it was in a very dilapidated state. I did not discover others that threw any light on the subject.

The population of the island, as stated by some travellers at one thousand souls, is evidently much underrated. From their wandering mode of life, and other causes, it was difficult, from any inspection of the island, to form a correct inference of the population of the whole; but the method I adopted was, at the conclusion of each day, to note the number of different individuals I had seen, and these I found, upon summing up, amount in all to above two thousand. This cannot, it is evident, comprehend half their number, for in several places they concealed themselves whenever we approached; and though my ramble led me to most parts of the island, yet there were necessarily many hills and remote valleys which I could not inspect. On the whole, I fix the amount at about four thousand. Two intelligent Arabs, who have resided on the island upwards of ten years, and have journeyed to many parts of it, tell me they consider this even below the actual number; but Arabs, where numbers are concerned, are but bad authorities. Comparing my calculation with the surface of the island, which amounts to about one thousand square miles, it gives four individuals to each square mile; which, when we reflect on the great proportion of bare rock its surface exhibits, is very considerable.

Although I made diligent search and constant inquiries, I was unable (with the exception of those which mark the stay of the Portuguese) to discover any vestiges or ancient monuments that would prove the island to have been peopled by a race further advanced in civilization than the present. I think, however, that there is reason to believe the population must have been at one time more numerous; and that the island was consequently better cultivated. It is impossible to ascertain at what period the number was reduced; but that they have not been exempt from contagion, or some other occasional scourge, appears evident from the existence of such a multitude of graves on every part of the island, many of which appear to have been constructed at the same time. On the other hand, that this period is somewhat remote, is equally evident, not only by the total disappearance of nearly all such traces of improvement on the face of the country, but by the present condition of the inhabitants. It must not be referred to the period immediately preceding the visit of the Wahábees, (as has been suggested in some discussions relating to the island); for those fierce sectaries confined their outrages, and the extent of their devastation, to Tamarida and its vicinity, and they did not attempt to pursue the inhabitants, who fled to the mountains on the first intimation of their approach.

# APPENDIX I.

The following Words and Phrases in the *Socotran* and *Arabic* are given as a specimen of the Language of that Island.*

| كلام العرب ARABIC. | كلام اهل جزيره سقطري SOCOTRAN. | | |
|---|---|---|---|
| طويل | *ríyau* | ريشو | Tall. Long. |
| قصير | *karhaï* | كرهي | Short. |
| ماي بحر | *Riyoh réh'n* | ريه رنهن | Salt Water. |
| ماي حلو | *Riyoh ḥálí* | ريه حالي | Sweet or Fresh Water. |
| ماي اشرب | *Riyoh larí* | ريه لري | Water to drink. |
| اكل | *ạstah* | استه | To eat. |
| بيت | *ḳár* | قار | A House. |
| بلاد | *chírhaï* | چيرهي | Town. |
| سيف | *eshukkó* | اشكو | Sword. |
| تفق | *bandúḳ* (Ar.) | بندوق | A Musket. |
| رصاص | *Raṣáṣ* (Ar.) | رصاص | Musket-ball (lead.) |
| حديد | *ḥaṣ-hen* | حصهن | Iron. |
| صفر | *ṣafạr* (Ar.) | صفر | Copper. |

* The Vowels are to be sounded as in *path, there, ravine, whole,* and *full*: the Consonants as in English, *ạ* as *u* in *cut, hut,* &c.; *aï* as *i* in *mine*; *au* as *ou* in *thou*; and the dotted letters somewhat more strongly than usual. Each letter has invariably the same sound; and the accents mark the long emphatic syllables.

| ARABIC. | SOCOTRAN. | | |
|---|---|---|---|
| حطب | *ṭérab* | طيرب | Wood. |
| نهار | *maṣh-hem* | مشهم | Day-time. |
| ليل | *aḥteh* | احته | Night-time. |
| قمر | *írah* | ايره | The Moon. |
| نجوم | *kókeb* (Ar.) | كوكب | The Stars. |
| شمس | *shíhen* | شيهن | The Sun. |
| تعال | *Ta'debah* | تعدبه | Come here. |
| روح | *Tetóhar* | تطوهر | Go away. |
| اجلس | *Istaháú(stuhúá?)* | استحاو | Sit down. |
| امشي | *ta'add* | تعد | Make haste. |
| ارقد | *eïdem* | ايدم | To sleep. |
| اوقف | *ḳaṣsah* | قصه | Scarce. |
| اليوم | *ḥar* | حر | To-day. |
| باكر | *ḳériri* | قيرري | To-morrow. |
| رجال | *éïj* | عيج | Male. |
| حرمة | *eïchah* | عيچه | Female. |
| ولد | *mobyáki* | مبياكي | Boy, or Male Infant. |
| متين | *'anạb* | عنب | Large Timber. |
| وصيم | *kaṭ'hen* | قطهن | Small Timber. |
| شهر | *shahr* (Ar.) | شهر | A Month. |
| شهرين | *terá b-shehreïn* | ترابشهرين | Two Months. |
| ثلاثه اشهر | *tata'ah shehr* | طلطة شهر | Three Months. |
| اربعة اشهر | *arb'ah shehr* | اربعه شهر | Four Months. |
| خمسه اشهر | *khúmis shehr* | خومس شهر | Five Months. |
| سته اشهر | *yítah* | يية شهر | Six Months. |
| سبعه اشهر | *yibí'ah shehr* | يبيعة شهر | Seven Months. |

| ARABIC. | SOCOTRAN. | | |
|---|---|---|---|
| ثمانيه اشهر | *tamání shehr* | ثماني اشهر | Eight Months. |
| تسعة اشهر | *sa'ah shehr* | سعه شهر | Nine Months. |
| عشرة اشهر | *'ashérah shehr* | عشيرة شهر | Ten Months. |
| حد عشر اشهر | *'aṭíré woṭát* | عطيري وطات | Eleven Months. |
| سنه | *aïnah* | اينه | A Year. |
| سنتين | *terí* | تري اينه | Two Years. |
| ثلاثه سنين | *ṭaṭa' aïhen* | ثلاثه ايهن | Three Years. |
| اربعه سنين | *arba'*— | اربع ايهن | Four Years. |
| خمسه سنين | *khémah*— | حيمه ايهن | Five Years. |
| سته سنين | *settah*— | سته ايهن | Six Years. |
| سبعه سنين | *yibí'ah*— | يبيعه ايهن | Seven Years. |
| ثمان سنين | *tamání*— | ثماني ايهن | Eight Years. |
| تسعه سنين | *sa'ah*— | تسعه ايهن | Nine Years. |
| عشرة سنين | *'asherah*— | عشرة ايهن | Ten Years. |
| حد عشر سنه | *ḥad-'asher*— | حدعشر ايهن | Eleven Years. |
| اثنه عشر سنه | *ethná'asher*— | اثنه عشر ايهن | Twelve Years. |
| ثلاثه عشر سنه | *telát'asher*— | ثلثعشر ايهن | Thirteen Years. |
| اربعة عشر سنه | *arba't'asher*— | اربعتعشر ايهن | Fourteen Years. |
| خمسة عشر سنه | *khamsat'asher*— | خمسة عشر ايهن | Fifteen Years. |
| ستعشر سنه | *sitt'asher*— | ستعشر ايهن | Sixteen Years. |
| سباتعشر سنه | *seb'at'asher*— | سبعتعشر ايهن | Seventeen Years. |
| ثمانتعشر سنه | *tmanet'asher*— | ثمانتعشر ايهن | Eighteen Years. |
| تستعشر سنه | *tis'at'asher*— | تسعتعشر ايهن | Nineteen Years. |
| عشرين سنه | *'ashrín*— | عشرين ايهن | Twenty Years. |
| ميه سنه | *miyah*— | ميه ايهن | One Hundred Years. |
| الف سنه | *alf*— | الف ايهن | One Thousand Years. |

| ARABIC. | | SOCOTRAN. | |
|---|---|---|---|
| خيط | *shúhaṭ* | شوهط | A Fishing-line. |
| مجدآر | *aḳlahah* | اقلهه | A Hook. |
| بلد | *bild* | بلد | Sounding-lead. |
| انجر | *barúṣí* | بروصي | Anchor. |
| سلسله | *sinsilah* (Ar.) | سلسله | A Chain for an anchor. |
| دقل | *daḳ'har* | دقحر | A Mast. |
| فرمن | *tarmál* | ترمل | A Yard. |
| شراع | *shíra'* (Ar.) | شيرع | A Sail. |
| ديره | *dírah* | ديره | A Compass. |
| فانوص | *fánúṣ* (Ar.) | فانوص | A Lantern. |
| بنديره | *Bindírah* (*Bandeira. Port.*) | نبديره | A Flag. |
| جبل | *Fed'han* | فدهن | A Hill, or Mountain. |
| حجار | *Ubeyem* | اوبهم | A Stone. |
| بعيد | *sherhoḳ* | شرهق | At a great distance. |
| قريت | *shélí* | شيلي | At hand. Close. |
| اشجار | *Shermuhem* | شرمهم | A Tree, Forest, &c. |
| الذره | *Makedhíra* | مقديره | Juwárí, (Holcus Sorghum.) |
| بر | *Baṛr* | بر | Corn, or Wheat. |
| طحين | *daḳíḳ* (Ar.) | دقيق | Flour. |
| خبز | *ezh-har* | ازهر | Bread, or Cakes. |
| تعال قريب | *túterdí* | قوتردي | Come here ! |
| روح بعيد | *tú'ad sherhoḳ* | توعد شرهق | Go away. |
| روح سوق | *ta'ad sóḳ* | تعدسوق | Go to Market or Bazaar. |

| ARABIC. | | SOCOTRAN. | |
|---|---|---|---|
| روح اليوم | *ḥeïrah tahr* | حيرة طهر | Go to-day. |
| تعال باكر | *ḳarírah tiḥdehn* | قريرة تحدهن | Come to-morrow. |
| زين | *dïyah* | دييه | Good. |
| شين | *diyá* | ديآ | Bad. |
| واحد | *káṭ* | قاط* | One. |
| اثنين | *tarawah* | تروه | Two. |
| ثلاثه | *ṭaṭa'ah* | ططعة | Three. |
| اربعه | *'arba'ah* | اربعه | Four. |
| خمسه | *ḥeïmish* | حيمش | Five. |
| سته | *yítah* | ايته | Six. |
| سبع | *yibí'ah* | يبيعه | Seven. |
| ثمان | *tamání* | ثماني | Eight. |
| تسع | *sa'ah* | سعه | Nine. |
| عشر | *'ashrí* | عشري | Ten. |
| تكلم | *ta'ashrí* | تعشري | Well-dressed. |
| عدل | *sawá* (Ar.) | سوا | Correct, proper, straight. |
| عوج | *kagh'hen* | قغهن | Crooked. |
| كثير | *Gaï* | كي | Plenty, numerous. |
| قليل | *Harar'hen* | حررهن | Few, scarce. |
| يابس | *Táshah* | تاشه | Dry. |
| بنت | *Ferhen* | فرهن | Daughter, or Female Child. |
| عجوز | *'ajúz* (Ar.) | عجوز | Old Woman. |
| شايب | *sheïb* | شيب | Old Man. |

* *táṭ* تاط (v. p. 211) or *ḥáṭ* حاط as in the Ethiopean dialects.

| ARABIC. | SOCOTRAN. | | |
|---|---|---|---|
| راس | *rí* | دي | The Head. |
| شعر | *shiff* | شف | The Hair. |
| جنون | *Terí'aïn tefrúz* | تري عين تفرز | The Eyebrows. |
| عين | *teï 'an* | طيعن | The Eyes. |
| حواجيب | *ḥaj-ḥar* | حجهر | The Forehead. |
| اذان | *edahn* (Ar.) | ادهن | The Ears. |
| خشم | *naḥír* | نحير | Nose. |
| براطم | *shíbah* | شيبه | The Lips. |
| ضروس | *meṭírmish* | مطيرمش | The Teeth. |
| لسان | *lishen* | لشن | Tongue. |
| رقبه | *naḥáshah* | نحاشه | The Throat. |
| كتف | *kaurí* | كري | The Shoulders. |
| ضهر | *ṭádah* | طاده | The Back. |
| بطن | *mír* | مير | The Stomach. |
| يد | *éyaṭ* | ايط | The Arm. |
| اصابيع | *'aṣábi'* (Ar.) | اصابع | The Fingers. |
| ظفور | *Dhafar* | ظفر | The Nails. |
| رجول [ارجل] | *sób* | صوب | The Feet. |
| رز | *arhaz* | ارهز | Rice. |
| سمن | *Hamí* | حمي | Ghí (clarified butter). |
| زبد | *ḳaṭmír* | تطمير | Butter. |
| حل | *ṣaléṭ* | صليط | Oil. |
| حليب | *húf* | حرف | New Milk. |
| دجاج | *dedáj* (Ar.) | دجاج | Fowls. |
| بيض | *beïḍh* (Ar.) | بيض | Eggs. |
| غنم | *ọrhen* | ارهن | Goats or Sheep. |

| ARABIC. | SOCOTRAN. | | |
|---|---|---|---|
| بقر | *elheïteïn* | الهيتين | Cows or Bullocks. |
| كلب | *kelb* (Ar.) | كلب | A Dog. |
| سنور | *yirbóḳ* | يربوق | The Civet Cat. |
| بوش | *Jemíher* | جمي هر | Camels. |
| غزال | *ṭahrír* | طهرير | Antelopes. |
| لحم | *teh* | ته | Meat. |
| سمك | *ṣódah* | صوده | Fish. |
| بصل | *Baṣṣ'hel* (Ar.) | بصهل | Onions. |
| صراج | *Sirúj* (Ar.) | صراج | A Light, of a candle, lamp, &c. |
| نار | *sheïwaṭ* | شيوط | Fire. |
| ابيض | *lebhem* | لبهم | White. |
| احمر | *ófir* | اوفر | Red. |
| ماي كثير | *Gí ríhó* | كي ريهو | Plenty of Water. |
| ماي قليل | *ríhó ḥararhen* | ريهو حررهن | Scarcity of Water. |
| بير | *eb-her* | ابهر | A Well. |
| حبل | *ket* | قيت | A Rope. |
| سكين | *sárí* | صاري | A Knife. |
| قلم | *ḳalam* (Ar.) | قلم | A Pencil. |
| دوايه | *dawáyah* (Ar.) | دوايه | An Inkstand. |
| قرطاس | *ḳarṭás* (Ar.) | قرطاس | Paper. |
| اكتب | *tó-kuttab* (Ar.) | توكتب | To write. |
| كتاب | *kitáb* (Ar.) | كتاب | A Book. |
| جلد | *jild* (Ar.) | جلد | Skin or Hide. |
| كمه | *kúfíyah* (Ar.) | كوفيه | A Cap. |
| عمامه | *'amámah* (Ar.) | عمامه | A Turban. |

| ARABIC. | | SOCOTRAN. |
|---|---|---|
| ثوب | *thób* (Ar.) | ثوب A Shirt. |
| حزام | *arádí* | ارادي A Sash, or Girdle. |
| وزرا | *makhfáf* (Ar.) | مخفاف Trowsers. |
| صندوق | *ṣandúḳ* (Ar.) | صندوق A Box or Chest. |
| كرسي | *kursí* (Ar.) | كرسي A Chair. |
| صحن | *ṣaḥau* (Ar.) | صحن A Plate or Dish. |
| مهفه | *merúḥah* (Ar.) | مروحه A Fan. |
| مدفع | *medfa'* (Ar.) | مدفع A Cannon. |
| باروت | *bárút* (Ar.) | باروت Gunpowder. |
| اصبر | *selúbah* | سلوبه Stop! Gently! |
| اعطي | *ṭáfa'ah* | طافعه To give. |
| اقبض | *telú* | تلو Take hold. |
| اخرج | *sheráhaḥ* | شراكح Go away. |
| ارجع | *taktátaḥ* | تكتاتح Come here. |
| ازبح | *taḥríz* | تحريز Kill. |
| اكثير | *kín* | كين Plenty of any thing. |
| امشي | *ta'óh* | تعوه Make haste! |
| اصحب | *'addah fahraï* | عده فحري To be on good terms. |
| آعدل | *tá ṣaḥḥ* (Ar.) | تاصح To behave properly. |
| انطف | *shemátó* | شماتو To converse. |
| اضبط | *'arr* | عر Take hold. |
| اصعد | *alleḥ* | الح To ascend. |
| انزل | *ta-ḳáfah* | تقافه To descend. |
| اجلس | *istaḥall* (Ar.) | استحل Sit down. |
| اقرا | *taḳári* (Ar.) | تقاري To read. |
| اعمر | *tanáfa'* (Ar.) | تنافع To mend. |

| ARABIC. | | SOCOTRAN. | |
|---|---|---|---|
| اخرب | *ta-nú'ash* (Ar.) | تنوعش | To spoil. |
| افرش | *ta-ásaf* (Ar.) | تاصف | To spread any Mat or Bed. |
| احسب | *ta ḥeïsib* (Ar.) | تحيسب | To count. |
| اشرط | *shálim* | شالم | To stake a bargain. |
| اضرب | *tawajjah* (Ar.) | توجه | To beat. |
| لاتضرب | *'en tájah* | عن تاجه | Do not strike. |
| اكسر | *ta-kása'* (Ar.) | تكاسع | To break. |
| لا تكر | *en-tafṭaf* (Ar.) | ان تفطف | Do not break. |
| لا تشرط | *'en elfirád* | عن الفراد | Make no agreement. |
| لا تعطي | *en tendeff* | عن تندف | Do not give. |
| ودا | *araḥ* | ارح | Remove or take away. |
| ودي | *araḥ yinúḳ* | ارح ينوق | To take any thing away. |
| لا تودي | *alà tiyé'i* | علي طيعي | Do not take away. |
| جيب | *nikyán* | نكيان | To bring. |
| لا تجيب | *alankah* | النكه | Do not bring. |
| زين | *díyah* | دييه | Good or well. |
| ما هو زين | *diya'* | ديع | No good. Bad. |
| اكل | *astà* | استا | To eat. |
| ما اكل | *an itúk* | ان اتوك | I have not eaten. |
| تقرب | *tú taher* | تو تهر | Come very close. |
| تبعد | *tetú saher* | تتو صهر | Go away to a distance. |
| آدمي | *Heïheï* | حيهي | A Man. |
| حي | *alḍháma'* | الظامع | Alive. |
| مات | *ṣámí* | صامي | Dead. |

| ARABIC. | SOCOTRAN. | | |
|---|---|---|---|
| شمس | *shohúm* | شهوم | The Sun. |
| ظلال | *míl'au* | ميلعو | A Roof, or Top, Awning, &c. |
| تكلم | *shemtar* | شمتر | Dressed well, or in good clothes. |
| قريب | *shíkah* | شيكه | Close to. |
| بعيد | *serhoḳ* | سرحق | At a distance off. |
| ايش عندك | *en mishaḳ* | انمشق | What have you got ? |
| صدق | *āmak* | آمك | True or Truth. |
| كذب | *tubạt* | تبت | Untrue—a Falsehood. |
| اخذ | *tez'en* | تزعن | Take hold. |
| لا تاخذ | *'en tez'en* | عن تزعن | Do not take hold. |
| لا تجلس | *taḳáṭa'* (Ar.) | تقاطع | Do not sit down. |
| لا توقف | *taṭúhar* | تطوهر | Do not stand. |
| ارقد | *t'shúf* | تشوق | To sleep. |
| اسبح | *tebáḥ (té-sobáḥ?)* | تباح | To wash. |
| انظر | *ta-ta'eïr* | تتعير | To look. |
| لا تنظر | *'en ta'eïr* | عن تعيّر | Do not look. |
| انكر | *teïber* | تيبر | Broken. |
| تعال قريب | *tekúde'n* | تكودعن | Come near. |
| روح بعيد | *tó'ad serḥoḳ* | توعد سرحق | Go away. |
| اعطي ماي | *abí ríhó* | ابي ريهه | Bring some water. |
| ماي بحر | *ríhó darnaham* | ريهه درنهم | Salt water. |
| اشتري | *astinjar* | استن جر | To buy. |
| بيع | *kathú'am* | كثوعم | To sell. |
| ابيع | *eshímah* | اشيمه | I will sell. |

| Date. | 4 A.M. | | | Sunrise. | | |
|---|---|---|---|---|---|---|
| | B. | T. | Winds. | B. | T. | Winds. |
| June 1 ......... | 29·36 | 88 | Calm. | — | — | — |
| 2 ......... | ·35 | 88 | — | 29·37 | 89 | Calm. |
| 3 ......... | ·28 | 88 | Southerly. | ·35 | 88 | E.S.E. |
| 4 ......... | ·30 | 85 | — | ·30 | 87½ | Variable. |
| 5 ......... | ·34 | 86 | S.S.E. | ·32 | 88 | S.E. |
| 6 ......... | ·33 | 82½ | S.E. | ·36 | 86 | — |
| 7 ......... | ·33 | 82½ | Lt. southerly. | ·31 | 83 | — |
| 8 ......... | ·33 | 81½ | Variable. | ·33 | 82 | Calm. |
| 9 ......... | ·34 | 82 | | | | |
| 10 ......... | ·34 | 82 | Strong S.W. | ·25 | 82 | S.W. |
| 11 ......... | ·28 | 86 | — | ·17 | 85 | — |
| 12 ......... | ·21 | 86½ | Vble. in gusts. | ·19 | 84 | S.S.W. |
| 13 ......... | ·20 | 85 | S.W. | ·20 | 84 | S.W. |
| 14 ......... | ·21 | 84½ | S.W. stg. gale. | ·21 | 86 | — |
| 15 ......... | ·24 | 83 | Mod. gale. | ·21 | 86 | Fresh gale. |
| 16 ......... | ·20 | 84 | — | ·22 | 87 | Mod. ditto. |
| 17 ......... | ·18 | 89 | Strong gale. | ·17 | 89 | — |
| 18 ......... | ·21 | 88 | Hard gale. | ·18 | 89 | — |
| 19 ......... | ·21 | 88 | Strong S.W. | ·21 | 88 | Fresh gale. |
| 20 ......... | ·22 | 89 | Light S.W. | ·22 | 89 | — |
| 21 ......... | ·24 | 88 | Fresh gale. | ·23 | 89 | Light airs. |
| 22 ......... | ·26 | 90 | Mod. S.W. | ·24 | 87 | — |
| 23 ......... | ·24 | 89 | Fresh S.W. | ·25 | 88½ | Fresh breeze. |
| 24 ......... | ·24 | 88 | Strong gale. | ·25 | 88 | Hard gale. |
| 25 ......... | ·19 | 89 | Hard gale. | ·24 | 88½ | — |
| 26 ......... | ·20 | 88 | Fresh gale. | ·19 | 81 | — |
| 27 ......... | ·30 | 89 | — | ·20 | 80 | — |
| 28 ......... | ·28 | 88 | — | ·30 | 87 | Fresh. |
| 29 ......... | ·22 | 88 | Mod. S.S.W. | ·30 | 87 | — |
| 30 ......... | ·22 | 88 | Strong S.W. | ·27 | 87 | — |
| July 1 ......... | ·20 | 86 | Hard gale. | ·21 | 87 | Hard gale. |
| 2 ......... | ·19 | 87 | Fresh breeze. | ·22 | 88 | S. Breeze. |
| 3 ......... | ·21 | 88 | — | ·21 | 88 | — |
| 4 ......... | ·22 | 88 | Hard gale. | ·21 | 88 | Hard gale. |
| 5 ......... | ·25 | 89 | Moderate. | ·26 | 88 | Fresh. |
| 6 ......... | ·24 | 87 | Hard gusts. | ·25 | 86 | Hard gale. |
| 7 ......... | ·19 | 68 | Mod. gale. | ·19 | 86 | Mod. ditto. |
| 8 ......... | ·12 | 88 | Hard gale. | ·19 | 87 | Hard ditto. |
| 9 ......... | ·21 | 87 | — | ·22 | 86 | Mod. ditto. |
| 10 ......... | ·20 | 85 | — | ·20 | 85 | Hard ditto. |
| 11 ......... | ·19 | 85 | — | ·19 | 85 | — |
| 12 ......... | ·26 | 85 | — | ·27 | 84 | — |
| 13 ......... | ·29 | 84 | — | ·29 | 83 | — |
| 14* ......... | ·30 | 80 | Fresh. | ·27 | 80 | Fresh monsn. |
| 15* ......... | ·20 | 79 | Stg. monsoon. | ·20 | 79 | — |
| 16 ......... | ·23 | 79 | — | ·23 | 79 | — |
| 17 ......... | ·29 | 80 | Moderate. | ·28 | 81 | — |
| 18 ......... | ·28 | 82 | — | ·29 | 82½ | Lt. & cloudy. |
| 19 ......... | ·29 | 82 | — | ·29 | 82 | Moderate. |

* Passage across to Bombay { On July 14, in latitude 13° 40′
— 15, — 14 47

| 8 A. M. | | | NOON. | | | 3 P. M. | | |
|---|---|---|---|---|---|---|---|---|
| B. | T. | Winds. | B. | T. | Winds. | B. | T. | Winds. |
| 29·34 | 87 | East. | 29·34 | 89 | Lt. variable. | 29·34 | 89 | E. N. E. |
| ·37 | 88 | North. | ·38 | 91 | Variable. | ·34 | 90 | E.S.E. |
| ·32 | 89 | Variable. | ·35 | 88 | North. | ·30 | 90 | N.W. |
| ·31 | 88 | W.S.W. | ·36 | 91 | S. E. | ·35 | 91 | S.E. |
| ·33 | 89 | S.W. | ·34 | 89 | S.E. by S. | ·30 | 87 | — |
| ·33 | 84 | Dense fog. | ·35 | 88 | Calm. | ·33 | 85 | West. |
| ·30 | 83 | — | ·30 | 85 | Foggy. | ·30 | 87 | Foggy. |
| ·25 | 82 | Southerly. | ·36 | 83 | Southerly. | ·30 | 86 | Southerly. |
| ·26 | 83 | S.W. | ·26 | 84 | Variable. | ·28 | 86 | Variable. |
| ·18 | 86 | Variable. | ·21 | 89 | Westerly. | ·17 | 91 | Light airs. |
| ·19 | 87 | Fr. S.W. | ·19 | 88 | S.W. | ·19 | 91 | Northerly. |
| ·20 | 86 | S. W. | ·20 | 89 | — | ·30 | 91 | Variable. |
| ·21 | 88 | — | ·22 | 91 | Fr. puffs. | ·20 | 91 | Strong. |
| ·21 | 88 | Fr. gale. | ·26 | 86 | — | ·22 | 90 | Moderate. |
| ·22 | 87 | Mod. do. | ·25 | 91 | Hard gale. | ·24 | 92 | — |
| ·19 | 88 | Fr. gale. | ·15 | 94 | Mod. ditto. | ·19 | 85 | Fresh. |
| ·22 | 87 | — | ·26 | 97½ | — | ·22 | 94 | Moderate. |
| ·23 | 89 | — | ·23 | 92 | — | ·22 | 93 | — |
| ·21 | 89 | — | ·20 | 92 | — | ·20 | 95 | — |
| ·22 | 89 | Lt. airs. | ·23 | 89 | — | ·20 | 94 | Lt. breeze. |
| ·24 | 89 | M. breeze. | ·24 | 93 | — | ·25 | 91½ | — |
| ·26 | 89 | Fresh puffs. | ·27 | 23 | Fresh. | ·26 | 97 | — |
| ·23 | 89 | Mod. gale. | ·26 | 92 | Mod. gale. | ·26 | 94½ | Moderate. |
| ·22 | 88 | Hard do. | ·22 | 88 | — | ·22 | 93 | Strong. |
| ·19 | 87 | — | ·22 | 90 | — | ·20 | 92 | Mod. gale. |
| ·24 | 87½ | Strong do. | ·26 | 92 | — | ·27 | 93 | — |
| ·31 | 87½ | — | ·34 | 91 | Lt. breeze. | ·33 | 92 | — |
| ·30 | 88 | — | ·31 | 90½ | — | ·28 | 94½ | Light airs. |
| ·26 | 87 | Mod. do. | ·25 | 91 | Moderate. | ·26 | 91½ | Moderate. |
| ·26 | 86 | Fresh gale. | ·29 | 90 | — | ·29 | 92 | — |
| ·21 | 87 | S. gale. | ·22 | 91 | Fresh. | ·21 | 93 | Fresh. |
| ·25 | 87 | Light. | ·25 | 87½ | — | ·21 | 90 | Light. |
| ·24 | 88 | S. breeze. | ·27 | 90 | Light. | ·26 | 92 | Moderate. |
| ·29 | 87 | — | ·26 | 89½ | — | ·26 | 92 | — |
| ·22 | 85 | H. gale. | ·23 | 90 | Fresh. | ·24 | 93 | — |
| ·20 | 87 | M. gale. | ·20 | 90 | Moderate. | ·19 | 90 | Fresh. |
| ·19 | 85 | Fresh. | ·21 | 89 | Hard gale. | ·21 | 92 | Strong. |
| ·26 | 86 | — | ·25 | 89 | Frh. breeze. | ·21 | 92 | — |
| ·20 | 85 | H. gale. | ·21 | 88 | Fresh gale. | ·23 | 89 | Fresh. |
| ·20 | 83 | — | ·22 | 87 | — | ·27 | 88 | — |
| ·28 | 82 | — | ·28 | 85 | — | ·29 | 86 | — |
| ·30 | 84 | — | ·29 | 86 | Moderate. | ·22 | 87 | Light off Deleshee |
| ·29 | 80 | Fr. mons. | ·29 | 81 | Fr. mons. | ·24 | 80½ | Fresh. |
| ·23 | 78 | — | ·23 | 82 | — | ·27 | 82½ | — |
| ·23 | 79 | — | ·23 | 82 | — | | 82½ | — |
| ·29 | 81 | — | ·29 | 82 | Moderate. | ·28 | 83½ | Moderate. |
| ·29 | 22½ | Moderate. | ·29 | 83 | — | ·28 | 83 | — |
| ·28 | 82½ | — | | | | | | |

* longitude 56° 58′; distance 955 miles to Bombay.*
— 60 27 — 673

| Date. | Sunset. | | | 8 P.M. | | |
|---|---|---|---|---|---|---|
| | B. | T. | Winds. | B. | T. | Winds. |
| June 1......... | 29·34 | 89 | N.N.E. | 29·35 | 88 | E.S.E. |
| 2......... | ·33 | 90 | Variable. | ·35 | 88 | — |
| 3......... | ·33 | 89 | Calm. | ·35 | 89 | Calm. |
| 4......... | ·33 | 91 | — | ·33 | 89 | — |
| 5......... | ·30 | 89 | N.E. | ·30 | 88 | East. |
| 6......... | ·31 | 86 | S.E. | ·32 | 88 | S.E. |
| 7......... | ·29 | 86 | — | ·29 | 89 | Calm. |
| 8......... | ·32 | 86 | Calm. | ·29 | 84 | S.E. |
| 9......... | | | | | | |
| 10......... | ·17 | 84 | West. | ·17 | 86 | West. |
| 11......... | ·19 | 89 | Southerly. | ·19 | 89 | Southerly. |
| 12......... | ·19 | 89 | Calm. | ·19 | 88 | S.W. |
| 13......... | ·20 | 91 | S.W. | ·20 | 91 | — |
| 14......... | ·20 | 91 | Strong puffs. | ·20 | 88 | Light airs. |
| 15......... | ·20 | 88½ | Lt. S.E. | ·22 | 92 | Moderate. |
| 16......... | ·22 | 92 | Moderate. | ·22 | 94 | Light. |
| 17......... | ·22 | 94 | — | ·18 | 89 | Moderate. |
| 18......... | ·18 | 90 | — | ·24 | 91 | — |
| 19......... | ·25 | 95 | — | ·21 | 91 | — |
| 20......... | ·22 | 93 | — | ·20 | 93 | Light. |
| 21......... | ·20 | 94 | Light. | ·21 | 91 | — |
| 22......... | ·22 | 91 | — | ·24 | 93 | — |
| 23......... | ·23 | 93 | — | ·27 | 93 | Variable. |
| 24......... | ·26 | 94 | — | ·27 | 93 | Moderate. |
| 25......... | ·26 | 93 | Moderate. | ·27 | 91 | Strong. |
| 26......... | ·22 | 92 | Fresh. | ·20 | 90 | Fresh. |
| 27......... | ·21 | 91 | — | ·20 | 90 | — |
| 28......... | ·29 | 91 | — | ·33 | 90 | Moderate. |
| 29......... | ·33 | 93 | Light airs. | ·29 | 91 | Calm. |
| 30......... | ·22 | 90 | Moderate. | ·24 | 89½ | Light airs. |
| July 1......... | ·29 | 91 | Light. | ·30 | 90 | Light. |
| 2......... | ·22 | 92 | Moderate. | ·21 | 90 | Fresh. |
| 3......... | ·25 | 88 | — | ·25 | 88 | — |
| 4......... | ·26 | 89 | Fresh. | ·25 | 89 | — |
| 5......... | ·24 | 90 | Moderate. | ·24 | 90 | Light. |
| 6......... | ·20 | 90 | Fresh. | ·22 | 88 | Moderate. |
| 7......... | ·20 | 89 | Strong. | ·20 | 89 | Fresh. |
| 8......... | ·20 | 89 | — | ·20 | 89 | — |
| 9......... | ·21 | 89 | Fresh. | ·22 | 88 | — |
| 10......... | ·27 | 89 | Strong. | ·19 | 88 | — |
| 11......... | ·27 | 88 | Light. | ·27 | 86 | Light. |
| 12......... | ·28 | 86 | Moderate. | ·26 | 85 | Moderate. |
| 13......... | ·22 | 84 | Fresh. | ·30 | 83 | — |
| 14......... | ·23 | 80 | Strong. | ·25 | 79 | — |
| 15......... | ·26 | 82 | Fresh. | ·23 | 80 | — |
| 16......... | ·26 | 81 | — | ·27 | 81 | — |
| 17......... | ·29 | 82 | Moderate. | ·29 | 82 | — |
| 18......... | ·29 | 83 | — | ·27 | 83 | — |
| 19......... | | | | | | |

| MIDNIGHT. | | | HYGROMETER. | | MEANS. | | |
|---|---|---|---|---|---|---|---|
| B. | T. | Winds. | Noon. | 8 P.M. | B. | T. | Winds. |
| 29·37 | 88½ | E.S.E. | ·42,0 | ·19,0 | 29 34 | 88½ | N.E. |
| ·33 | 88 | S.S.E. | ·31,0 | ·39,5 | 29 35 | 89 | E.N.E. |
| ·30 | 89 | Variable. | ·45,0 | ·34,0 | 29 33 | 89 | N.E. |
| ·32 | 89 | S.S.E. | ·32,0 | ·18,0 | 29 33 | 89 | W. |
| ·31 | 87 | — | ·29,0 | ·17,0 | 29 32 | 87 | E. |
| ·30 | 84 | — | ·19,0 | ·20,7 | 29 33 | 85 | S.S.E. |
| ·30 | 82 | Mod. S. | ·22,0 | ·18,0 | 29 31 | 85 | Southerly. |
| ·29 | 83 | Southerly. | ·16,0 | ·66,2 | 29 33 | 83 | — |
| | | | | | — | — | — |
| ·17 | 83 | S.W. b. W. | ·36,0 | ·94,0 | 29 26 | 83 | S.W. |
| ·17 | 88 | W. b. S. | ·87,0 | ·80,3 | 29 18 | 88 | — |
| ·19 | 88 | S.W. | ·81,0 | ·52,0 | 29 19 | 88 | — |
| ·20 | 88 | — | ·90,0 | ·84,0 | 29 20 | 88 | — |
| ·20 | 88 | Lt. airs. | ·97,0 | ·70,0 | 29 20½ | 88 | — |
| ·20 | 88 | Moderate. | ·78,0 | ·70,0 | 29 23 | 87 | S.S.W. |
| ·27 | 88 | Variable. | ·88,0 | ·92,0 | 29 24 | 89 | — |
| ·18 | 88 | Mod. gale. | ·78,0 | ·78,0 | 29 18 | 91 | — |
| ·29 | 83 | — | ·74,0 | ·74,0 | 29 19 | 88 | S.W. |
| ·27 | 89 | Calm. | ·77,0 | ·68,0 | 29 22 | 90 | — |
| ·21 | 89 | Lt. airs. | ·76,0 | ·49,0 | 29 21 | 89 | — |
| ·20 | 90 | — | ·69,0 | ·52,0 | 29 22 | 91 | — |
| ·26 | 89 | Fr. puffs. | ·74,0 | ·59,0 | 29 23 | 90 | — |
| ·27 | 91 | Mod. gale. | ·72,0 | ·87,0 | 29 25 | 92 | — |
| ·27 | 91 | — | ·82,0 | ·87,0 | 29 25 | 91 | S.W. b. S. |
| ·20 | 88½ | H. gale. | ·64,0 | ·80,0 | 29 24 | 89 | S.W. |
| ·22 | 89 | Fr. gale. | ·79,0 | ·73,0 | 29 21 | 87 | — |
| ·29 | 88 | Mod. gale. | ·72,0 | ·72,0 | 29 26 | 90 | W.S.W. |
| ·29 | 89 | Moderate. | ·84,0 | ·54,0 | 29 31 | 89 | S.W. |
| ·28 | 88½ | — | ·82,0 | ·68,0 | 29 26 | 90 | S.S.W. |
| ·24 | 89 | St. breeze. | ·82,0 | ·75,0 | 29 23 | 88 | S.W. |
| ·25 | 88 | Moderate. | ·82,0 | ·71,0 | 29 26 | 88 | — |
| ·24 | 90 | Light. | ·80,0 | ·79,0 | 29 22 | 88 | — |
| ·26 | 88 | — | ·83,0 | ·60,0 | 29 23 | 89 | — |
| ·25 | 89 | Moderate. | ·86,0 | ·91,0 | 29 24 | 89 | — |
| ·26 | 89 | Light. | ·74,0 | ·92,0 | 29 26 | 89 | — |
| ·22 | 89 | Moderate. | ·98,0 | ·101,0 | 29 23 | 91 | — |
| ·22 | 87 | Fresh. | ·81,1 | ·87,0 | 29 20 | 88 | — |
| ·22 | 87 | — | ·76,0 | ·81,1 | 29 20 | 88 | — |
| ·20 | 88 | — | ·81,1 | ·74,0 | 29 24 | 88 | — |
| ·18 | 87 | — | ·75,0 | ·74,5 | | | |
| ·28 | 85 | Hard. | ·68,0 | ·66,0 | | | |
| ·17 | 85 | — | ·65,0 | ·65,0 | | | |
| ·29 | 81 | — | ·55,0 | ·33,0 | | | |
| ·25 | 79 | — | ·18,0 | ·27,0 | | | |
| ·23 | 80 | Fr. mons. | ·17,0 | ·17,0 | | | |
| ·30 | 81 | — | ·21,0 | ·20,0 | | | |
| ·29 | 80½ | Moderate. | ·21,0 | ·20,0 | | | |
| ·29 | 83 | — | ·21,0 | ·22,0 | | | |

THE END.

Printed by J. L. Cox and Sons, 75, Great Queen Street,
Lincoln's-Inn Fields.

Lightning Source UK Ltd.
Milton Keynes UK
UKHW021948310120
357983UK00008B/65

9 780342 259595